MW01147558

Compact Guide: Venice is the ultimate quick-reference guide to this fascinating destination. It tells you all you need to know about Venice's attractions, from the grandeur of St Mark's Square to the elegance of the Grand Canal, from the backwaters of Cannaregio to the islands of the Lagoon, and from the bustle of the Rialto Bridge to the treasures of the Frari.

This is one of 130 Compact Guides, combining the interests and enthusiasms of two of the world's best-known information providers: Insight Guides, whose innovative titles have set the standard for visual travel guides since 1970, and Discovery Channel, the world's premier source of nonfiction television programming.

Rialto
*Poscheria
S Giacomo dall'Orio
Ponte

Discovery CHANNEL

APA PUBLICATIONS L
Part of the Langenscheidt Publishing Group

Insight Compact Guide: Venice

Written by: Wolfgang Thoma
English version by: David Ingram
Updated by: Adele Evans
Edited by: Jeffery Pike
Photography by: Glyn Genin
Additional photography and cover picture by: Ros Miller
Design: Maria Lord
Picture Editor: Hilary Genin
Maps: Dave Priestley
Design Concept: Carlotta Junger

Editorial Director: Brian Bell
Managing Editor: Tony Halliday

CONTACTING THE EDITORS: As every effort is made to provide accurate information in this publication, we would appreciate it if readers would call our attention to any errors and omissions by contacting:
Apa Publications, PO Box 7910, London SE1 1WE, England.
Fax: (44 20) 7403 0290
e-mail: insight@apaguide.demon.co.uk

Information has been obtained from sources believed to be reliable, but its accuracy and completeness, and the opinions based thereon, are not guaranteed.

© 2002 APA Publications GmbH & Co. Verlag KG Singapore Branch, Singapore.

First Edition 1996. Second Edition 2002
Printed in Singapore by Insight Print Services (Pte) Ltd
Original edition © Polyglott-Verlag Dr Bolte KG, Munich

Worldwide distribution enquiries:
APA Publications GmbH & Co. Verlag KG (Singapore Branch)
38 Joo Koon Road, Singapore 628990
Tel: (65) 865-1600, Fax: (65) 861-6438

Distributed in the UK & Ireland by:
GeoCenter International Ltd
The Viables Centre, Harrow Way, Basingstoke,
Hampshire RG22 4BJ
Tel: (44 1256) 817987, Fax: (44 1256) 817-988

Distributed in the United States by:
Langenscheidt Publishers, Inc.
46–35 54th Road, Maspeth, NY 11378
Tel: (1 718) 784-0055, Fax: (1 718) 784-0640

www.insightguides.com

Venice

Introduction

Places

Culture

Travel Tips

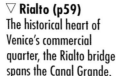

▽ **Rialto (p59)**
The historical heart of Venice's commercial quarter, the Rialto bridge spans the Canal Grande.

△ **Canal Grande (p39)**
Lined with splendid Renaissance palaces, a boat trip along the Grand Canal is an unforgettable experience.

▷ **San Rocco (p69)**
The Scuolo Grande de San Rocco is world-famous for its paintings by the Venetian artist Tintoretto, especially his moving *Crucifixion*.

△ **Murano (p99)**
A 'mini Venice', famous for its fine glassware.

▷ **The Salute (p76)**
This huge church is one of Venice's most famous landmarks.

◁ **The Frari (p66)**
One of Venice's greatest churches, full of artworks.

△ **Cannaregio (p79)** One of the least-explored areas of the city, the lovely canals and quiet back streets hide a number of attractions, including the Ghetto and the Palazzo Ca' d'Oro.

△ **St Mark's Basilica (p21)** The mighty facade of San Marco and its campanile (bell tower) dominate St Mark's Square. Home to countless works of art, and the burial place of St Mark, the interior is visually overwhelming.

△ **The Accademia (p77)** Home to the most inportant and complete collection of 14th–18th century Venetian paintings.

▷ **The Doges' Palace (p30)** The impressive palace of the rulers of Venice overlooks Piazza San Marco and the Lagoon.

Wonder of the World

In the popular imagination, Venice offers a kaleidoscope of images, from romantic gondolas to garish Murano glassware, from crumbling palaces on the Grand Canal to masked revellers at the Venetian Carnival. Summer presents the bustling splendour of Piazza San Marco while winter is swathed in mystery: the mist-laden, monochrome curtain of a city out of season. Then, the city conjures up the melancholy of Visconti's haunting *Death in Venice*, based on Thomas Mann's novel.

Any gloom is soon dispelled by *cichetti* (snacks and appetisers) or a fishy risotto. Luminous Venetian painting embraces Canaletto's stately majesty, Titian's vibrant explosions of colour and Tintoretto's mastery of light and shadow. Private Venice harbours its own pleasures, from secluded backwaters to mildewed churches or the soporific sound of boat horns drifting over the canals.

For more than a millennium, the Republic of Venice used all its strength to repel unwelcome invaders. Today it welcomes the foreign hordes with open arms: one of the world's greatest maritime powers has become one of the world's greatest tourist attractions. Its sheer uniqueness makes it a wonder of the world. No other Western city has so many historic buildings built on water; few other cities have so successfully straddled East and West, with glittering architectural treasures from both worlds.

Venice needed no structural alterations in order to accommodate modern traffic; cars simply have to turn back once they reach Piazzale Roma. As a result, Venice is unsullied by modernity, an act of foresight on the part of the city's founders. Not for nothing is Venice known as La Serenissima, 'the most serene' city, the title bestowed on it by its Republican rulers.

LOCATION AND SIZE

Situated at the northwestern end of the Adriatic Sea, Venice lies on an archipelago in a crescent-shaped lagoon some 51km (32 miles) in length. At 1 metre (3¼ft) above sea-level, Greater Venice

Earning and spending
Once-wealthy Venice, where around half the population are now employed directly or indirectly in the tourist trade, has the lowest per capita income of any city in Veneto, although consumer prices are the highest in Italy.

Opposite: the Grand Canal towards La Salute
Below: gondolas at the Molo
Bottom: crowds on St Mark's Square

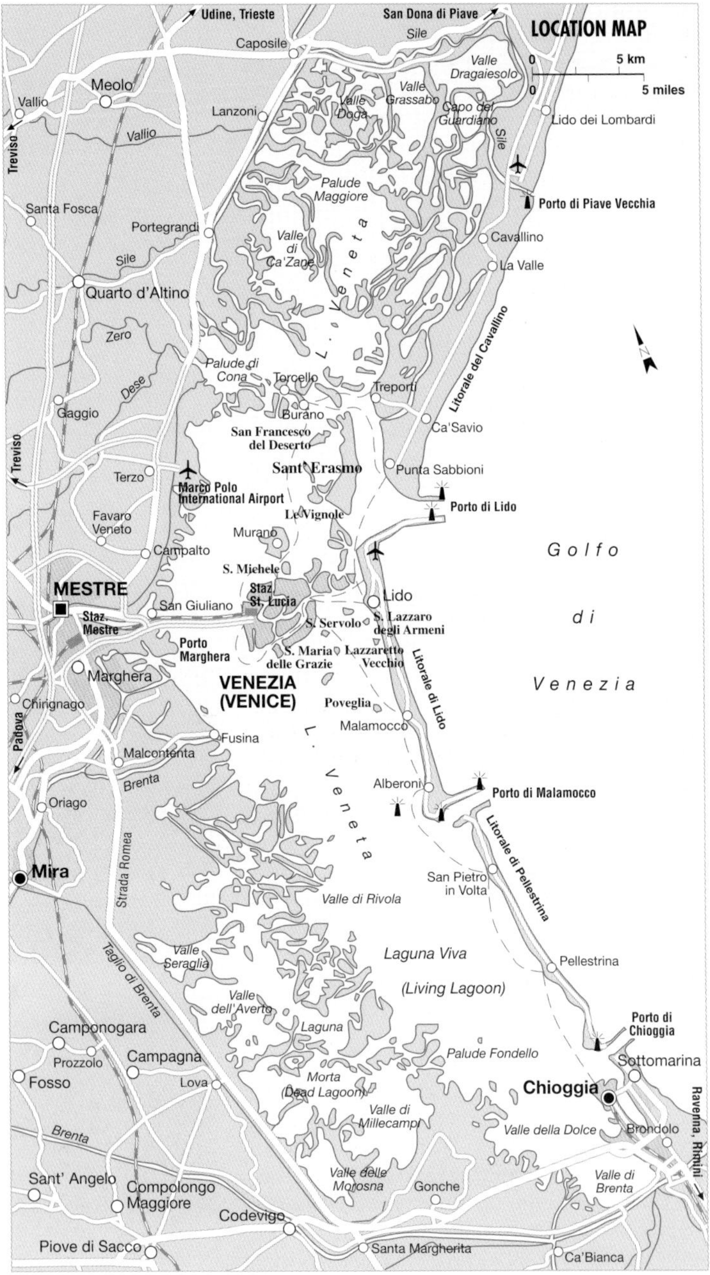

LOCATION MAP

0 — 5 km
0 — 5 miles

Udine, Trieste
San Dona di Piave
Caposile
Sile
Valle Dragaiesolo
Meolo
Vallio
Lanzoni
Valle Doga
Valle Grassabo
Capo del Guardiano
Lido dei Lombardi
Sile
Vallio
Treviso
Santa Fosca
Portegrandi
Palude Maggiore
Porto di Piave Vecchia
Cavallino
Sile
Valle di Ca'Zane
La Valle
Quarto d'Altino
Zero
Litorale del Cavallino
Palude di Cona
Torcello
Treporti
Gaggio
Dese
Burano
Ca'Savio
Terzo
San Francesco del Deserto
Sant'Erasmo
Marco Polo International Airport
Le Vignole
Punta Sabbioni
Porto di Lido
Favaro Veneto
Murano
Campalto
S. Michele
Golfo
MESTRE
Staz. St. Lucia
Lido
San Giuliano
S. Servolo
S. Lazzaro degli Armeni
di
Staz. Mestre
Porto Marghera
S. Maria delle Grazie
Lazzaretto Vecchio
Venezia
Marghera
VENEZIA (VENICE)
Poveglia
Litorale di Lido
Chirignago
Malamocco
Padova
Fusina
L. Veneta
Malcontenta
Brenta
Alberoni
Porto di Malamocco
Oriago
Mira
Litorale di Pellestrina
San Pietro in Volta
Valle di Rivola
Valle Seraglia
Laguna Viva
Taglio di Brenta
Valle dell'Averto
(Living Lagoon)
Pellestrina
Laguna
Porto di Chioggia
Camponogara
Palude Fondello
Prozzolo
Campagna
Morta (Dead Lagoon)
Sottomarina
Fosso
Lova
Chioggia
Brenta
Valle di Millecampi
Valle della Dolce
Ravenna, Rimini
Sant' Angelo
Compolongo Maggiore
Valle delle Motosna
Gonche
Brondolo
Valle di Brenta
Piove di Sacco
Codevigo
Santa Margherita
Ca'Bianca

stands on 118 islets in this shallow lagoon. The city of Venice itself is linked by 160 canals and criss-crossed by more than 600 bridges.

The shallow waters of the Venetian lagoon are protected from the open sea by the Litorale del Cavallino promontory in the north, the Chioggia-Sottomarina promontory in the south, and in between are a line of sandbanks or *lidi*. These sandy islets are home to small settlements, of which the best known is the Lido, built as a fashionable seaside resort in the 19th century.

Like natural sluices, the three gaps of Porto di Lido, Porto di Malamocco and Porto di Chioggia all connect with the sea, which is essential for shipping as well as for the lagoon's ecological balance. But the sea also represents a threat to Venice because of the risk of high tides; the last devastating flood was in 1966.

Venice's strategically unique position resulted in the development of an equally unique city within the lagoon. Harbours that had silted up, such as the one at Ravenna further south on the Adriatic, made the Venetians realise the threat to their own city, and they soon redirected the Brenta, Sile and Piave rivers with estuaries in the lagoon. Such medieval foresight meant that Venice never silted up, and remained a port.

RISE OF A MARITIME POWER

Cut off from the mainland, its secure position guaranteed, and facing out towards the sea and the East, Venice developed a brisk, long-distance trade with Byzantium, a relationship which flourished from the 5th century onwards. The city exported ships, salt and fish, and imported sought-after consumer goods in return: spices, silks and exotic luxuries. The craft traditions of Byzantium, unchanged since antiquity, catered to the needs of Europe's medieval masters via the Venetian clearing house. The city also manufactured its own glassware and built ships for trade and war.

Securing the shipping routes brought coastal fortifications and colonisation in its wake. Venice controlled the islands of Rhodes, Cyprus, Crete

Refuge from barbarians
From the 5th century AD, Huns (led by Attila), Goths, Ostrogoths, Lombards and Franks all streamed across the Alps into the Friulian Plain. But the swampy marshes and the mudflats of the Venetian lagoon did not appeal to the invading barbarians. Thus the low-lying lagoon islands became a sanctuary for the local inhabitants, fleeing from the onslaught. By 466, refugees from Padua, Verona, Aquileia and other cities had founded 12 settlements on the islands, and had elected tribunes to coordinate common actions and policy.

Pope Alexander III gives Doge Ziani a sword

Scuola di San Giovanni Evangelista

and Corfu, with Corfu remaining Venetian until the end of the Republic in 1797. Marco Polo (1254–1324), the great Venetian adventurer, travelled throughout the Far East and helped open up trading links between Asia and the West. As for trade with the Black Sea and North Africa, the safe harbours of Koron and Modon at the southern exit of the Adriatic were known as the 'Eyes of the Republic'.

In its heyday, Venice was undisputed ruler of the Adriatic and the eastern Mediterranean. In 1420 it was the richest city in the world, and 200 years later, after the lion's share of territorial possessions had gone to Turkey, Venice still possessed more wealth than the great powers of Central Europe. It was this prosperity that led to such a flowering of the arts in the 17th and 18th centuries, after the initial Renaissance bloom had faded.

Long before the fall of Constantinople (1453) Venice had been expanding across to the mainland, creating neighbouring colonies and distant caravan routes. It was almost as if it sensed the impending loss of its maritime trade. The Peace of Lodi (1454) secured it the routes across the Alps and into Central Italy. Nevertheless, the discovery of the New World created new patterns of trade, and Venice was ultimately sidelined.

THE DOGES AND THEIR REPUBLIC

None of Venice's burgeoning power would have been possible without the security engendered by the Venetian Republic. The Republic, run by an unbroken line of doges for more than a thousand years, represented the rock beneath the shifting sands of Venetian fortunes. The role of doge (from the Latin *dux*, leader) was an institutionalised version of a Byzantine governorship.

The position was not hereditary, thus removing the threats posed by monarchy or feudalism. Instead, the doge acted as the public representative of enlightened patrician rule, a position which gradually evolved into a figurehead role. The doges, backed by the checks and balances provided by the Republican constitution, oversaw a period of great prosperity and artistic patronage. Until its abolition in 1797, the Venetian constitution occupied a unique place in European history, at once the staunch defender of the ruling class and the guarantor of civic duty.

LEGACY OF A WORLD POWER

Venice was a world maritime power for centuries, and the effects are obvious, from the magnificent Doge's Palace to the late Byzantine flowering of San Marco. This was a cosmopolitan city of Levantine, Bohemian, Greek and Slav merchants. Architecturally, too, Venice became a melting-pot, with a bias for Byzantine richness over Renaissance purity of line. The palaces flanking the Grand Canal were built over a span of around 500 years.

Venice set a precedent in house design: the floor of each palazzo was open, because the city's secure location made fortifications unnecessary. On the ground floor, where boats were moored, was the warehouse; above was the *piano nobile*, the main floor, graced with *saloni* and anterooms. Standing sentinel outside the palazzi are *paline*, the mooring poles bedecked in the colours of the original patrician residents.

In financial matters, Venice was the acknowledged world leader and has bequeathed us much

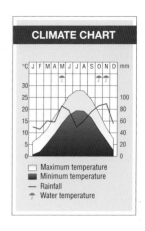

CLIMATE CHART

- ☐ Maximum temperature
- ■ Minimum temperature
- — Rainfall
- ☂ Water temperature

Below: a proud emblem
Bottom: palazzi along the Grand Canal

basic banking terminology. Many expressions commonly used in Venetian trade with the Orient also found their way into European languages, including such words as arsenal, coffee, ghetto, magazine and marzipan.

VENICE IN PERIL

Below: a city on the water
Bottom: treading the boards
on St Mark's Square

The centuries-old problem of Venice sinking was halted by measures taken in the 1970s against industrial communities disturbing the balance of the lagoon. But the city is still plagued by other problems, ranging from pollution from the industrial zones of Mestre and Marghera to flooding and depopulation. A further blow to the city's image was the destruction of the Fenice opera house by fire in January 1996. This jewel of a theatre will rise again, as it did after the fire of 1836, but inevitably its reconstruction will divert funds from other vital projects.

Venice has always been threatened by floods: the combination of an area of low pressure in Northern Italy, a strong southeasterly wind and simultaneous tides can send masses of water from the Adriatic into the lagoon. On 14 November 1966 the city was flooded for 13 hours up to a depth of nearly 2m (over 6ft). An appeal was launched, and in 1992 the government finally released funds for the so-called 'Progetto Mosè'

(Moses Project) involving the construction of huge mobile flood protection barriers at the Porto di Lido, Porto di Malamocco and Porto di Chioggia. But after a viability study by a team of international experts, the controversial project was put on hold by the government at the end of 1998 and its future now hangs in the balance.

VENICE TODAY

Venice is by no means a living museum. The inhabitants are noted for their tricky dialect, fierce independence, sense of irony and stoical approach. Theirs is a spirit born out of the slow pace of Venetian life and a lingering nostalgia for past greatness. It is personified by the sultry yet cool Venetian aristocracy or the offhand approach of the city gondoliers. Yet this public mask also conceals a carnivalesque temperament, a sense of fun which is given free rein at festivals.

In its heyday, the city of Venice had 200,000 inhabitants, a figure that fell to 90,000 at the end of the Republic. By 1995 the population had dwindled to a mere 73,000. This emigration has not been entirely voluntary: the city does not have enough rented accommodation, and flats are too expensive for most locals. Also, building restoration costs in Venice are almost double those of mainland Mestre. As a consequence, more Venetians are moving to Mestre and commuting to work. While Venice lives off industry on the mainland, its islands depend on tourism.

Some 12 million tourists spend at least one day in the city each year, and Venice has long toyed with the idea of introducing a quota system. However, only a tiny proportion of visitors stay overnight: most depart in the evening. This is a time when the city breathes again. Yet out of season Venice has much to offer, apart from the riotous pre-Lenten Carnival. Venice is just as intriguing in winter, retaining the cheerful attitude to life that is so characteristic of its inhabitants. And in the murky depths of winter fogs, one of the best ways to restore cheer is to enjoy a *grappa*, the famous drink originally distilled in Venice.

Street talk
The Venetian dialect differs from standard Italian in many respects. With echoes of Spanish, a street is usually called *calle* and a canal *rio*. (The status of *canale* is reserved for the Grand Canal and one or two others.) There is only one *piazza* in Venice – St Mark's, with its two adjacent *piazzette* – and only one *piazzale* – Piazzale Roma, the car park. All the other squares are *campi* or, if they're tiny, *campielli*.

Washing day in Castello

HISTORICAL HIGHLIGHTS

c 1000BC The first settlers in the area arrive from the Aegean or Asia Minor.

2nd century BC The Venetia area becomes a Roman colony. Many of the lagoon islands are already inhabited.

401 AD Alaric the Goth attacks the city of Aquileia: citizens take refuge on the islands of Venice.

425 Refugees from Padua form a colony on Rivo Alto island – later to be known as Rialto, the centre of modern Venice.

452 Attila the Hun destroys Aquileia: more refugees flee to Venice. Island communities begin working together.

539 Venetian fleet helps Byzantines to take Ravenna; Venice is rewarded with trading privileges in the East.

697 Paoluccio Anafesta is elected the first doge. The Venetian fleet is the largest in the Adriatic.

752 Lombards take Ravenna, effectively driving the Byzantines out of Italy. Venice now controls the seas.

810 Threatened by Charlemagne's son Pepin, Venetians move the capital from the island of Malamocco to Rialto, where they resist a six-month siege.

1000 In response to pirate attacks, Venice sends a victorious expedition to the Dalmatian coast.

1082–5 Victory over the Normans, who posed a threat to Venetian access to the Adriatic.

1094 San Marco is consecrated.

1104 The Arsenale is founded.

1177 Venice intercedes in the controversy between the Emperor and the Pope: Barbarossa and Alexander III meet in San Marco.

1202–4 The Fourth Crusade ends with the capture of Constantinople. Venice attains the height of its colonial power: it controls nearly half of the Byzantine Empire, the Cyclades and Crete, and shipping routes as far as the Black Sea.

1254 Marco Polo is born in Venice.

1271 At age 17, Marco Polo sets off from Venice, travels via Baghdad, Persia (Iran) and Afghanistan to reach the court of the Mongol prince Kublai Khan. As the prince's adviser, he then travels throughout the Far East – the first European to visit China – and helps open up trading links between Asia and the West.

13th and 14th centuries The creation of *scuole*, the charitable confraternities or guilds which bestowed so much on the city in terms of artistic patronage.

1310–14 Tiepolo and Querini plot to oust Doge Gradenigo.

1339 War with Verona over control of shipping routes: Venice gains Treviso, Conegliano and Castelfranco.

1355 Doge Marin Falier is beheaded for treason.

1378–81 War with Genoa ends in a Venetian victory at Chioggia. The Peace of Turin reaffirms Venetian supremacy.

1405 Venice takes Verona from Milan.

1423 Doge Francesco Foscari begins Venetian expansion to Bergamo, Brescia and parts of Cremona.

1453 The Ottomans conquer Constantinople; trading routes with the Orient are cut off.

1454 The Peace of Lodi: Venice secures the routes across the Alps and into Central Italy. Its territory now comprises the Po Valley, Lake Garda, the Alps and Istria.

1492 The loss of Black Sea trade is followed by the discovery of America.

1498 Vasco da Gama discovers the sea route to India via the Cape of Good Hope. Venice no longer monopolises trade with India and declines as a world power.

16th century Venice prospers, acting as a trade clearing house between Europe and Asia. This is the golden age of Venetian painting, with Bellini (1430–1516), Titian (1488–1576), Tintoretto (1518–94) and Veronese (1528–88).

1508 The 'League of Cambrai'. France, Spain, the Emperor, the Pope and the Italian city-states form an alliance against Venice, which surrenders its Italian mainland colonies.

1570 Cyprus falls to the Turks. Venice and the Western powers defeat the Turks at the Battle of Lepanto (1571), but this alters nothing.

17th century The House of Habsburg (Austrian and Spanish line) and the threat from Turkey remain the two polarising forces in Venetian politics. Venice lives on its accumulated wealth.

1699 Venice reconquers the Peloponnese.

1718 Peace of Passarowitz: Venice relinquishes all its colonial possessions; Austria and Turkey reach an agreement. Venice is no longer a world power, but a mere state.

18th century Venice becomes a city of adventurers and gamblers. The decadence of the time is accurately portrayed by writers Giacomo Casanova and Carlo Goldoni and the genre painters Pietro Longhi (1702–84), Francesco Guardi (1712–93) and Canaletto (1697–1768).

1797 The Napoleonic army surrenders Venice without a fight to its arch-enemies, the Habsburgs.

1805 Venice becomes part of Napoleon's Kingdom of Italy.

1815 The Congress of Vienna returns Venice to Austria.

1848 The revolutionary leader Danielle Manin sets up a provisional republican government, but it falls the following year.

1866 Venice becomes part of a unified Italy after Prussian forces defeat the Austrians at Sadowa.

1914–18 Italy declares war on Austria; the Venetian mainland becomes a World War I battleground. More than 600 bombs are dropped on the city but most monuments survive.

1946 Foundation of the Republic of Italy.

1958 Giuseppe Roncalli, Patriarch of Venice, becomes Pope John XXIII.

1966 Venice is severely damaged by floods. International appeal launched to save the city.

1994 Approval of the Mosè (Moses) Project, a mobile dam to prevent flooding.

1996 La Fenice opera house is destroyed by fire.

1998 Mosè Project is put on hold after environmental protests.

BERNARDO BELLOTTO
1722 1780

Map on page 19

Museum ticket

One ticket for the 'Musei di Piazza San Marco' includes admission to the Museo Correr, the Palazzo Ducale, the Museo Archeologico Nazionale and the Sale della Biblioteca Nazionale Marciana. Buy your ticket at any of these.

Below: coffee on the Piazza
Bottom: St Mark's facade

1: Piazza San Marco

Piazza San Marco – San Marco Basilica – Doge's Palace

Connoisseurs insist that the best way to approach San Marco for the first time is by water. If this isn't possible, there is also a very good view to be had when entering the arcades of the **Ala Napoleonica ❶** (those not on foot should disembark at the San Marco-Calle Vallaresso landing-stage), where the least attractive part of the entire complex is at your back.

There was a gap in the architecture there right up until 1810, when Napoleon ordered it to be closed – he referred to St Mark's Square as the 'finest drawing-room in all Europe', but still felt that a rear wall had to be added.

MUSEO CORRER

This Napoleonic wing today contains the entrance to the ★★ **Museo Correr** (open Apr–Oct: daily 9am–7pm; Nov–Mar: daily 9am–5pm). The collection here includes cultural and historical artefacts (documents, costumes, coins), an art gallery with 14th- to 16th-century masterpieces (mainly Venetian) and a collection of works by Canova, and also the special Museo di Risorgimento section, documenting the resistance against

the Austrian occupation during the 19th century.

The two wings of the building on the north side of the piazza are known as the *procuratie*, formerly the offices of the city's most important administrative officials, the procurators. On the site of the previous building here, which was Byzantine in style, the **Procuratie Vecchie** (Old Procurators' Offices) ❷ were built between 1480 and 1517. Designed by Mauro Codussi, they were constructed by Bartolomeo Bon. The arcades still have a Byzantine flavour; the arches are not imitation, but actually an Early Renaissance novelty.

Scamozzi started on the construction of the **Procuratie Nuove** (New Procurators' Offices) ❸ opposite in 1582, and the building was completed by Longhena around 1640.

Star Attraction
● Museo Correr

Gondolas at the Molo, with the Column of St Mark, viewed from the Campanile

OLD LIBRARY

The Procuratie Nuove were not modelled on Byzantium but instead on the **Libreria Vecchia** (Old Library) ❹ just around the corner, now part of the Biblioteca Nazionale Marciana. Begun in 1537 by Jacopo Sansovino, it was completed after his death by Scamozzi, and marked a turning-point in Venetian architecture. The Byzantine and Gothic styles had served their purpose, and the classically oriented ideals of the Renaissance were now coming into their own. The Old Library has a long, graceful facade arcaded on two storeys; the richly decorated frieze is pierced by attic windows. This new formal language introduced by Sansovino became an object of study not only in Venice but all over Europe.

The library is well worth visiting during temporary exhibitions or by appointment (tel: 041-520 8788). The staircase with its white and gold stucco emulates the Scala d'Oro in the Doge's Palace *(see page 34)*. On the ceiling is Titian's fresco of *Wisdom*. The Sala Dorata (Golden Hall) has a gold ceiling separated into seven sections, each containing three medallions: seven painters had a contest

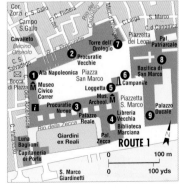

here, supervised by Titian, and the winner was Paolo Veronese (6th row). Five of the 12 paintings of philosophers on the walls are by Tintoretto. The glass cases contain the most valuable of the Old Library's ancient books; there are 750,000 altogether, and they are stored in the former Zecca (Mint), the wing facing the Molo.

*Below: the Campanile
Bottom: the Loggetta gateway*

The **Museo Archeologico Nazionale** is housed in the Ala Napoleonica in part of the Procuratie Vecchie and Biblioteca Nazionale Marciana. It has Greeek, Roman, Egyptian and Assyrian-Babylonian sections.

THE CAMPANILE

The ★ **Loggetta** ❺, with its three arches and ornate attic, resembles a rather over-wide Roman city gate, and is also by Sansovino. Towering above it is the ★ **Campanile** ❻ (open Jun–Sept: daily 9am–9pm; Oct–May: 9.30am–4.15pm). The oldest structure in the square, it was begun in the 9th century. After several construction phases between the 12th and 14th centuries, the 98-m (322-ft) high tower was completed in 1514. On 14 July 1902 the campanile collapsed, causing little damage to other buildings and no human casualties; its reconstruction was officially opened on St Mark's Day (25 April) in 1912. The view from the campanile across the lagoon – and sometimes as far as the Alps – is justly famous.

Three imposing-looking flagstaffs stand in front of the church: this is where the flag of St Mark is still hoisted during festivals. The bronze pedestals are by Alessandro Leopardi (1505).

CLOCK TOWER

A popular sight are the *due mori* (Two Moors), the bronze figures who strike the hours up on the ★★ **Torre dell'Orologio** (Clock Tower) ❼. Codussi had originally planned the tower as the final section of his Procuratie Vecchie, and the bronze figures of the Two Moors were cast in 1497, as was the clock, which shows not only the time of day but also the phases of the moon and the passage of the sun through the zodiac. The lion in front of the stars was added in 1755, along with the upper storey.

Star Attractions
• Torre dell'Orologio
• St Mark's Basilica

ST MARK'S BASILICA (SAN MARCO)

At the eastern end of the Piazza is ★★★ **St Mark's Basilica** ❽ (Basilica, Pala d'Oro and Treasury open: Mon–Sat 9.45am–4.30pm, Sun 2–4.30pm; Gallery and Museum: daily 9.45am–5.30pm; last entry 30 minutes before closing).

In 828, two Venetian merchants stole the relics of St Mark from Alexandria, brought them to Venice and presented them to the doge. The building that now houses them was consecrated in 1094. It was modelled after the Church of the Apostles in Constantinople, later destroyed by the Turks when they captured the city. Its ground plan is a Greek cross with four arms of equal length. The two-storey facade is divided into five arcades, the middle ones of which were emphatically decorated as the main portal.

> **Angelic approval**
> The theft of St Mark's remains from Alexandria was given some spurious legitimacy by a legend which tells that, on a voyage from Aquileia to Rome, the Evangelist took refuge from a storm on an island in the Venice lagoon. There an angel spoke to him in a dream: *Pax tibi, Marce evangelista meus. Hic requiescet corpus tuum* ('Peace be with you, Mark, my Evangelist. This will be your final resting-place') – thus conveniently justifying the young state's claim to the relics.

BRONZE HORSES

The city's rapid rise to power after the success of the Fourth Crusade allowed the facade to be adapted to contemporary 13th-century taste, namely Romanesque. The carrier sections of the

These famous bronze horses, now on view in the St Mark's Museum, were stolen from Constantinople

Map on page 19

Mark Three

The first San Marco basilica, a wooden chapel hastily erected to house the Evangelist's relics, was consecrated in 832. It was damaged by fire in 976, during the bloody insurrection that also burnt down the Doge's Palace and assassinated Doge Pietro Candiano IV at the church door. Both the church and the palace were rebuilt in their original form, and the second San Marco was consecrated in 978. But the chapel was soon regarded as inadequate and was demolished in 1063, to be replaced by the present building. This was commissioned by Doge Domenico Contarini, who issued the order 'to make the chapel the most beautiful ever seen'.

Gothic icing on the Basilica facade

lower arcades were replaced by playful double pillars which break up the facade. More booty from Byzantium followed in the shape of the four ★★★ **bronze horses** on the loggia. Then the baptistery and St Isidore's chapel were added, along with the domes. The appearance of the facade at that time has been preserved in the mosaic of the first arcade on the left.

GOTHIC ICING

During the first half of the 15th century the facade was adorned with some Gothic icing: pointed arches made the arcades higher, and the building's brick exterior was faced with fine marble and decorated with works of art from all over the world.

Five doorways lead from the front of the building into the narthex; four of them have bronze doors, the fifth is glass. The main facade is in two orders, each of five arches, with the emphasis on the central arch, the main portal. Its ★ **bronze doors** with their lions' heads came from Byzantium in the 11th century. The main outer arch has 14th-century carvings showing Venetian trades – in sharp contrast to the *Last Judgement*, a neoclassical mosaic that was added in 1836. The sculpture below is Romanesque (12th- and 13th-centuries) and depicts the Months (soffit), the Virtues and Beatitudes (outer face), and symbolic representations of animals (smallest arch). In the lunette is an expressive Romanesque marble carving of the *Dream of St Mark* (13th-century).

The side portals are also richly decorated with mosaics showing how the relics of St Mark were brought to Venice. The mosaic on the far left is the only one dating from the time of the Romanesque reconstruction (1260–70). It is the earliest known representation of the building's exterior, with the bronze horses already in place.

NORTH FACADE

The north facade, facing the Piazzetta dei Leoncini, was probably the last to be finished. The first arch has a 7th-century relief of Christ and the disciples as lambs. A bas-relief between the first two arches shows Alexander the Great being transported to heaven by two griffins (10th-century Byzantine). All three arches are decorated with an assortment of geometrical figures and mysterious animals and shapes.

The last of the four arches is the 13th-century Porta dei Fiori (Flower Portal); the beautifully carved pointed arches enclose a nativity scene, a masterpiece of Venetian Romanesque. Beyond the projecting wall here is the porphyry sarcophagus of Daniele Manin, who led the rebellion against Austrian rule that was crushed in 1849. At the southwest corner of the facade is the Pietra del Bando, a stump of a porphyry column from which the decrees of the Signoria were promulgated from 1256 onwards.

SOUTH FACADE

The south facade, formerly open to the Molo, has been closed for some time now because of the reconstruction of the Cappella Zen. Between the two upper arches is a 13th-century Byzantine mosaic of the Madonna in prayer. The two isolated pillars in front of the baptistery door, with their Oriental motifs, are a rare example of Syrian carving of the 4th century.

The massive wall that leads to the Doge's

Star Attraction
● Bronze horses

Below: St Mark's domes
Bottom: the Last Judgement

Map on page 26

Below: a mosaic in the narthex
Bottom: an intarsia floor

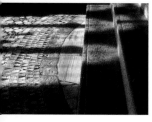

Palace is decorated with polychrome marble intarsia; there may once have been a fortified tower on this site, forming part of the old Doge's fortress. The sculptured group on the corner is known as the *Tetrarchi*. The four figures (4th-century Egyptian) are thought to represent Diocletian and three other Roman emperors.

THE NARTHEX

The centre doorway leads into the **narthex** (atrium), which originally lined three sides of the church's actual interior; the side facing the Piazzetta was closed and was given a new liturgical function as the Cappella Zen and the baptistery. The oldest part, which dates back to the beginning of the building, can be seen in the section containing the elaborate central doorway: the austere pillars, arches, niches and mosaics betray their Byzantine origin. The bronze doors are early 12th-century, and were modelled after the ones on the right-hand portal (11th-century Byzantine). The bronze door in front of the Cappella Zen [Y] resembles the central doorway on the exterior facade: Byzantine art (6th-century).

The ★ **intarsia floors** of the narthex are 11th- and 12th-century. In front of the centre portal, a red marble slab marks the spot where Barbarossa did obeisance before Alexander III in 1177, at the height of the investiture controversy. The *St Mark in Ecstasy* mosaic (1545) in the semi-dome is the work of Francesco and Valerio Zuccato, based on a sketch by Lorenzo Lotto. The ceiling of the narthex was originally flat; the domes were vaulted in the 13th century, which is also when the mosaic floor was added. The mosaics of the domes and arches are on themes taken from the Old Testament: [A] *Creation and the Fall of Man*, [B] the *Story of Noah and the Flood*, [C] the *Tower of Babel*, [D] the *Story of Abraham*, [E] the *Story of Joseph*, [F] *Joseph is Sold to Potiphar*, [G] *Joseph Rules Egypt*, [H] the *Story of Moses*. These mosaics clearly reveal how Venetian artists succeeded in freeing themselves from the severity and formality of the Byzantine tradition, and developed their own dynamic and highly imaginative mosaic style.

Before leaving the narthex and entering the interior of San Marco proper, the numerous pillars should not be missed: their capitals are miniature masterpieces.

INTERIOR SPLENDOURS

The ★★ **interior** of the basilica is breathtaking: the interplay of the domes and arches creates a dynamic rhythm, while the actual shape of the ground plan with its four arms of equal length arrests this architectural movement and calms it again. San Marco is a compelling and harmonious blend of the dynamic and the static, of tranquillity and movement. Before any details can be distinguished, one is almost dazzled by the apparently infinite number of mosaics on their gold backgrounds – covering more than 4,000sq m (43,000sq ft) of space.

The main Dome of the Ascension [**I**] shows Christ being carried by four angels, and Mary by two; the 12 Apostles frame the picture. The 16 Virtues of Christ are depicted between the windows; the four Evangelists are in the four pendentives. The dome above the altar [**II**] shows the Religion of Christ as foretold by the Prophets; the Virgin stands between Isaiah and Daniel; the sym-

Star Attraction
● San Marco interior

> **Hierarchy**
> The holy figures depicted in glorious mosaics in San Marco are placed around the building according to the original medieval iconographical scheme: Christ is uppermost, high in the cupola; beneath him are the angels and Apostles, with the Story of St Mark; then, below them, the pillars and arches are decorated down to ground level with stories of various select saints.

The Dome of the Ascension

San Marco in print

The travel writer Jan Morris described San Marco as 'a Barbaric building like a great Mongolian pleasure pavilion'. Earlier, American author Henry James wrote of 'the molten colour that drops from the hollow vaults and thickens the air with its richness'. He recalled the tabernacles 'whose open doors disclose a dark Byzantine image spotted with dull, crooked gems'.

bols of the four Evangelists are in the spandrels.

In the Dome of the Pentecost [**III**] the mosaics depict the Triumph of Faith: the Descent of the Holy Spirit, with tongues of fire inspiring the 12 Apostles and, between the windows, the Converted Nations. The mosaics in these three 12th-century domes are artistically the most valuable, although several of them have had to be renewed over the centuries and many have been redone in the style of the 16th and 17th centuries.

I Above the centre portal, *the Saviour between the Virgin and St Mark* (13th-century, restored); in the arch, *Scenes from the Apocalypse* (16th-century and modern); also a *Last Judgement* based on sketches by Jacopo Tintoretto (16th-century).

J *The Passion*, from the Kiss of Judas until the Crucifixion (13th-century).

K *Scenes from the Life of Christ*, based on sketches by Jacopo Tintoretto (16th-century).

L *The Passion, the Agony in the Garden, Deeds of the Apostles* (13th-century).

M *Christ and the Apostles; the Deeds of the Apostles* (13th- to 16th-century).

N *Christ Pantocrator*, based on sketches by Tintoretto (16th-century).

O *Scenes from the Life of Christ* (12th- to 13th-century).

P *Deeds of John the Evangelist*; in the centre, a Greek cross; the *four Fathers of the Church* in the pendentives (late 12th-century).

Q Several saints particularly popular with the Venetians: *St Nicola, St Clemente, St Biagio, St Leonardo* (13th-century).

ST MARK'S

0 — 20 m
0 — 20 yds

THE ICONOSTASIS

The many art treasures in St Mark's, whether plundered, donated or made in Venice, are concentrated in the choir around the presbytery (*presbiterio*). It is somewhat higher than the rest of the church because of the crypt (*cripta*) beneath it. The ★ **iconostasis** separates the priests from the ordinary people. The liturgical reform of the second Vatican Council (1962–4) placed a rather ugly wooden podium in front of the screen so that Mass could be celebrated 'closer to the people'. But the podium hides almost all the stylobate with its 16 marble arches, from the previous 10th-century church. The artistic polychrome marble structure is crowned by a series of sculptures: grouped around the dominant cross in the middle are the *Virgin, St John the Evangelist and the 12 Apostles* – a work by Jacobello and Pierpaolo delle Masegne (1394).

On the right platform made of porphyry and marble, supported by nine pillars of various exotic marbles, the newly elected doge was presented to the public. On the left-hand side are two ★ **pulpits**. The lower, octagonal one has an impressive marble parapet and is supported by 11 pillars. The higher one is remarkable for its design: seven narrow columns support the pulpit, which consists of five cylindrical posts; above it, on six red marble columns, is a little Oriental cupola.

Below: a detail from the dome mosaics
Bottom: looking down the nave to the iconostasis

THE CHOIR

To the right of the iconostasis, the way leads inside the choir; the two tribunes opposite one another with bronze reliefs by Sansovino (16th-century)

Map on page 26

Medieval masterpiece
The Pala d'Oro is one of the most remarkable works ever produced by medieval gold-smiths. It consists of beautifully worked gold, set with 300 sapphires, 300 emeralds, 400 garnets, 100 amethysts, as well as handfuls of rubies and topazes. They all accompany 157 tiny, intricate scenes in enamelled rondels and panels.

were for singers and musicians. The high altar gained its present-day appearance from the restoration phase of 1834–6. The ★★ **columns** supporting the baldachin are particularly delight-ful: they are decorated with sculpture from top to bottom, with motifs taken from the Life of Christ and of the Virgin; their origin is uncer-tain, and they have been dated between the 6th and 13th centuries. The altarpiece provides a view of the sarcophagus of St Mark; the bronze lamps are 16th-century.

THE PALA D'ORO

Beyond the high altar is the unique ★★★ **Pala d'Oro**, with its precious stones, old gold and enamel, which was originally planned to go in front of the altar. Doge Pietro Orseolo (976–78) commissioned it in Constantinople; over five cen-turies it was enlarged and enriched.

The six *Scenes from the Life of Christ* in the upper section came from Byzantium in 1209. The lower section is the work of Venetian artists (1345): in the centre, the Pantocrator, surrounded by the four Evangelists and flanked by three rows of Prophets, Apostles and Angels. Square niches with enamels, worked in the *cloisonné* technique, depict episodes from the lives of Christ, the Vir-gin and St Mark (1105).

A detail of the Pala d'Oro

The apse of St Mark's has three niches: the altar in the middle one is decorated by four spiral-shaped columns, and the tabernacle by Sansovino bears a bronze relief of the Saviour. The remarkable sacristy door in the left-hand niche is also by Sansovino; and through the golden grille in the right niche, the doge could watch the church unobserved. The mosaic in the apse shows Christ Pantocrator (1506). The saints between the windows below are remains of mosaics dating from the time the church was first built (11th century).

Star Attraction
● Pala d'Oro

Below: the apse Pantocrator
Bottom: the Baptistery font

SIDE CHAPELS

R Cappella di Sant'Isidoro (St Isidore's chapel). 14th-century mosaics illustrating the life of St Isidore; Gothic altar (14th-century) containing the saint's relics.

S ★ Cappella della Madonna dei Mascoli. 15th-century mosaics illustrating the *Life of the Virgin*; the altar by Bartolomeo Bon is encased in splendid marble.

T Mosaics illustrating the *Life of the Virgin* (12th- and 13th-century).

U Cappella della Madonna Nicopeia. A 10th-century icon of the Virgin, taken to Venice after the sack of Constantinople in 1204; the name means 'victory-bringer'.

V Altare del Sacramento. An eternal flame stands as a reminder that the relics of St Mark were found again after the fire of 976; the floor mosaic shows where they were found in 1094.

W In the nave pier, a large bas-relief of *Madonna con Bambino* (Madonna and Child, also known as *Madonna del Bacio*, Madonna of the Kiss, since it has been worn away by the kisses of the faithful).

X Battistero (Baptistery). Font designed by Sansovino (1546) with reliefs (Evangelists; *Scenes from the Life of John the Baptist*); opposite the entrance, the tomb of Doge Andrea Dandolo (1343–54) who had the baptistery installed in the former ambulatory here; mosaic decoration (14th-century).

Y Cappella Zen (Zeno chapel). Impressive tomb

Maps
on pages
26, 19, 35

Museum views

In the gallery of the **Museo Marciano** (Museum of St Mark) are some very valuable works connected with the history of the basilica: tapestries, hangings, paintings, mosaic fragments and the original four gilded bronze horses that used to adorn the exterior of the Basilica. The gallery also provides a good close-up view of the Apocalypse mosaic (16th-century) and of the roof of the narthex; steps here lead along the walls as far as the transepts. It is worth studying the floor of the basilica from up here: it was laid when San Marco was first built, and its slight undulations give a good impression of just how shaky the soil is beneath.

The Bridge of Sighs, between the Doge's Palace and Prison

(1505–21) of Cardinal Zeno; the sarcophagus, baldachin (canopy), statue of the cardinal and the other figures are all cast in bronze. On the altar is a Lombardesque *Madonna della Scarpa* (Madonna of the Shoe); according to legend, the Virgin presented a poor man with a shoe that turned to gold. In the vault, *Scenes from the Life of St Mark*.

Z ★★ **Tesoro** (Treasury). Most of its precious possessions were captured during the sack of Constantinople in 1204; 11 niches contain 110 gold and silver reliquary caskets, studded with precious stones. The incense burner or coffer is in the shape of a Byzantine church; the so-called 'Chair of St Mark', a marble monolith of Oriental origin (6th- to 8th-century); valuable Byzantine Gospel covers. Despite the fact that much of it was melted down in 1797 at the end of the Republic, the rich store of booty here is still very impressive.

DOGE'S PALACE (PALAZZO DUCALE)

Adjoining the basilica is the ★★★ **Doge's Palace** ❾ (open Apr–Oct: daily 9am–7pm, Nov–Mar: daily 9am–5pm; last admission 2 hours before closing).

At the beginning of the 9th century the seat of the doges was shifted from the Rialto to San

Marco. The first Doge's Palace burnt down in 976, the second in 1106, and the third had to make way for a new building before the visit by Barbarossa in 1177. Hardly anything remains of the four previous structures in today's building, although the massive square pedestal on the left of the entrance might once have been part of a corner tower.

Star Attractions
● **San Marco Treasury**
● **Doge's Palace**

Construction of the present building began in 1340. Fresco painter Guariento was summoned in 1365, which means that the first section of the building facing the harbour basin was probably completed by then. Doge Michele Steno (1400–04) commissioned the intarsia ceiling in the Great Hall, and the magnificent windows facing the lagoon were added. On 30 July 1419 the Great Council *(Maggior Consiglio)* held its first session.

Below: the palace facade
Bottom: the lion of St Mark

The decoration of the Palace – each arcade of the portico supports two arches of the loggia, ornamented with quatrefoil roundels – formed the basis for numerous variations throughout the city. The high wall is broken up by broad, pointed-arch windows (the two facing the bridge are original). This three-level facade, which perfectly integrates structure, material and decoration, has been likened to an altar frontal in rich brocade. The balconied window in the middle was built by Jacobello and Pierpaolo Delle Masegne.

SECOND PHASE

The second construction phase was the result of dilapidation: in 1424 the decision was made to demolish and rebuild the wing as far as the church in the style of the wing at the Molo, which had already been completed. This was done by 1438, and architects Giovanni and Bartolomeo Bon, father and son, crowned their achievement with that supreme example of the Late Gothic style, the ★★ **Porta della Carta** (1438–42), with its group showing Doge Foscari (1423–57) kneeling in front of the lion of St Mark.

This graceful gateway filled in the last gap, and the new facade of the Doge's Palace was complete after more than a century of building work. The

Map on page 35

36 capitals are superb examples of medieval carving. On the corners of the palace are some fine statues, including the *Drunkenness of Noah, Adam and Eve*, and the *Judgement of Solomon*. These three corners are crowned by archangels: *Raphael*, representing trade, *Gabriel* (peace) and *Michael* (war). The Venetians' favourite attribute, *Justice*, crowns the balconied windows in the middle (Alessandro Vittoria, 1577–79). The marble ornamental crenellations on top of the facade are not just a feature of the Doge's Palace; they are repeated on the Procuratie, and extend around the square.

Below: Adam and Eve Bottom: the courtyard from the top of the Giant's Staircase

Once the exterior was complete, construction work carried on inside the building: the Arco Foscari, a groin-vaulted triumphal arch, was added as a continuation of the Porta della Carta and extended as far as the courtyard before its final completion under Doge Cristoforo Moro (1461– 72). The sculptures of *Adam and Eve* are the work of Antonio Rizzo (the 1476 marble originals are inside the palace; the bronzes here in the courtyard are copies).

THIRD PHASE

The third phase of building followed a conflagration that destroyed the east wing next to the canal in 1483. Antonio Rizzo was commissioned to rebuild it, and he was followed by Pietro Lombardo in 1498 and then by Scarpagnino, both of

whom carried out his plans. The Renaissance had arrived: the loggia with its pointed arches on the first floor is still Gothic, but the round arches everywhere else now set the trend. Rizzo's ★★ **Scala dei Giganti**, the staircase used by the doges during coronation ceremonies, is named after Sansovino's colossal sculptures of Mars and Neptune. The exterior was completed around 1525, and now the interior needed to be decorated.

Stonemasons from Tuscany, Lombardy and Venice had worked for a century on the building's Gothic wings and now shared the interior decoration with the greatest painters of the age. Bellini, Vivarini, Carpaccio, Titian, Veronese, Tintoretto and many others decorated the Doge's Palace – and all their work was lost in two fires (1574 and 1577). The stonemasons were more fortunate. The damage was repaired under the supervision of Antonio da Ponte and Bartolomeo Monopola.

Towards the end of the 17th century the Doge's Palace finally received its present-day appearance, and the 18th century preserved it. After Venice was incorporated into the Kingdom of Italy (1866), the new state ordered restoration work on the Doge's Palace. It was finally returned to the City of Venice in 1923. Venice now had its palazzo back again. With its two facades, the Doge's Palace is still the finest example of florid Gothic architecture in the city.

PALACE TOUR

The Scala dei Giganti leads to a fine loggia with a good view of the courtyard. The two richly ornamented bronze well-heads date from 1554–59. The Facciata dell'Orologio, the section of facade with the clock, between the stair and the entrance hall, is the work of Bartolomeo Monopola (1603–14). The small church of St Nicholas next door stands empty.

The small section of courtyard on the other side of the Scala dei Giganti is known as the Cortile dei Senatori (Senators' Courtyard), and is a fine Renaissance work by architects Spavento and Scarpagnino (1507).

Star Attraction
● Scala dei Giganti

Palace plan
The palace reflects (on a grand scale) the Venetian Gothic style used for residential buildings and shops: open arcades below, and a magnificent loggia above. As in most Venetian houses, the ground floor was used for various subsidiary purposes, including storage. The first floor *(piano nobile)* comprised assembly rooms and the doge's residence, and the upper storey contained the state rooms and council chambers.

Palace columns

Map on page 35

Around the Palace
There is no single recommended route for tours of the Doge's Palace, because different sections of the building are often closed for restoration. Signs displayed in each of the rooms list their contents, but it is also worth buying the official guide book.

The Scala d'Oro

ROOMS AND THEIR TREASURES

A ★ Scala d'Oro (Golden Staircase). Designed in 1555 by Sansovino; named after the magnificent marble and gilded stucco decoration in the vaults.

B Sala degli Scarlatti (Robing Room), where officials wearing scarlet togas would collect the doge. Intarsia ceiling in gold on blue background (1505); superb marble chimneypiece by Antonio and Tullio Lombardo (1502).

C Sala dello Scudo (Shield Room). This is where the reigning doge's shield and weapons were kept; the armour belonging to the last doge, deposed in 1797, can still be seen. The maps date from 1540, and were restored along with the rest of the room in 1761.

D Sala Grimani. Wooden Lombardesque ceiling decorated with the coat-of-arms of Doge Grimani (1595–1605); sculpture frieze.

E Sala Erizzo. Lombardesque ceiling (early 16th-century); frieze with putti (17th-century); coat-of-arms of Doge Erizzo (1631–46) set above the marble chimneypiece.

F Sala degli Stucchi (Stucco Room). Fine stucco work with caryatids dating from reign of Doge Grimani (1595–1605); copy of Tintoretto's *Henry III of France*; from the window, a fine view of the apse of San Marco.

G Sala dei Filosofi (Philosophers' Room). Doge Foscarini (1762–63) adorned the walls here with 12 philosophers from the cycle in the Old Library *(see page 20)*; they were restored to their original place in 1929. Above the door leading to the staircase is *St Christopher* by Titian (1523–24).

H Doge's residence. Magnificent ceiling intarsias and marble chimneypieces; *Pietà* by Giovanni Bellini (1470); *The Damned in Purgatory* by Hieronymus Bosch; *Lion of St Mark* by Carpaccio (1516).

I Sala degli Scudieri (Palace Guardroom).

J Atrio Quadrato. Fine wooden ceiling (1560) with painting by Tintoretto.

K Sala delle Quattro Porte (Room of Four Doors). The four doors were designed by

Palladio (1574–76); magnificent stucco ceiling with caryatids; ceiling frescoes by Tintoretto; wall frescoes depicting historic events; in front of the window, *Neptune Offering Venice the Riches of the Sea* by Tiepolo (1740).

L Sala dell'Anticollegio. Magnificent stucco and marble, and frescoes designed by Palladio (1576); paintings by the three contemporaries Tintoretto, Veronese and Bassano.

M ★ **Sala del Collegio.** Considered one of the finest rooms in the palace, because of the harmonious mix of decoration and fine art. Superb ceiling by Francesco Bello, including a fine

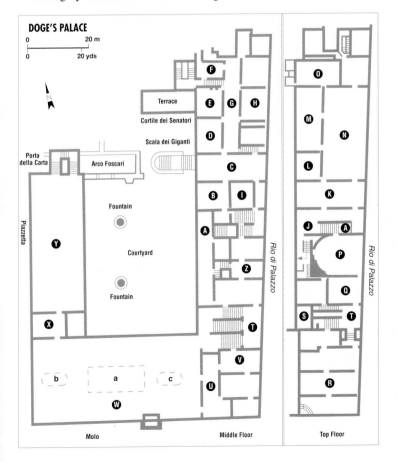

DOGE'S PALACE

Map on page 35

Below: Tintoretto's 'The Apotheosis of Venice'
Bottom: Veronese's 'The Battle of Lepanto'

series of paintings by Veronese (1575); on the wall above the throne, the *Battle of Lepanto* by Veronese; wall paintings by Tintoretto, including portraits of several doges.

N Sala del Senato. Another fine ceiling; the centrepiece is *The Triumph of Venice* by Jacopo and Domenico Tintoretto.

O Chiesetta. The doge's private chapel, also used by the senators; designed by Scamozzi (1593); a *Madonna* by Sansovino (1486–1570).

P Sala del Consiglio dei Dieci. The seat of the Council of Ten, founded in 1310, reconstructed in 1533–50.

Q Sala della Bussola (Compass Room). Antechamber to Council of Ten; on the right of the farther door, a *Bocca di Leone* (lion's mouth), a box in which secret denunciations were placed; paintings by the Veronese school; marble chimneypiece by Sansovino.

R Armeria (Armoury). The Council's private armoury, now a museum of ancient weapons.

S Sala degli Inquisitori (Inquisition Room). A council of three carried out interrogations here; a staircase connected it with the torture-chamber and the cells beneath the roof. On the ceiling, *Return of the Prodigal Son* by Tintoretto.

T Scala dei Censori (Censors' Staircase).

U Andito del Maggior Consiglio (Corridor of the Great Council). On the left wall, works by Domenico Tintoretto, and opposite, by Palma Giovane.

V Sala della Quarantia Civil Vecchia (Old Courtroom). This is where the tribunal held its sessions for civil cases. The interior decoration is 17th-century. The adjoining room, the Sala del Guariento, contains the remains of a huge fresco (destroyed by fire) of the *Coronation of the Virgin* by Guariento, which he painted for the Great Council.

W ★★★ **Sala del Maggior Consiglio** (Hall of the Great Council). This hall is where the parliament of patricians used to sit, sometimes as many as 1,600 of them. They ratified laws and elected the highest officials of the Republic. On 2 April 1849, during the Austrian occupation, *resistenza ad ogni costo* (resistance at all costs) was proclaimed here. The magnificent gold ceiling (1578–85) frames 15 frescoes. The centre panel (**a**) by Tintoretto: *Venice as Queen Gives an Olive Branch to Doge Nicolò da Ponte* (1578–85); on the window side, by Jacopo Palma il Giovane (**b**) *Venice Welcoming the Conquered Nations Around Her Throne*; and the counterpart to this by Paolo Veronese (**c**) ★ *Venice Surrounded by Gods and Crowned by Victory*. The 21 wall paintings, depicting historical scenes, are by the workshops of Tintoretto and Veronese; on the window wall is Veronese's *Triumph of Doge Contarini after the Victory over Genoa at the Battle of Chioggia*; Tintoretto's *Paradise*, one of the world's largest oil paintings, can be seen opposite it. Above the wall canvases is a long frieze showing the first 76 doges, painted by Domenico and Jacopo Tintoretto; the portrait of Doge Marin Faliero, who was deposed and then executed in 1355, has been replaced by an inscription.

X   Sala della Quarantia Civil Nuova (New Courtroom). A finely carved ceiling; no paintings.

Y   ★★ **Sala dello Scrutinio**. This room was used to record the votes of the Great Council for the new doge. The frieze of doge portraits is continued in this room up to the end of the

Star Attractions
● **Sala del Maggior Consiglio**
● **Sala dello Scrutinio**

> **Torture tour**
> The 'secret' tour (**Itinerario segreto**) shows visitors lesser-known parts of the Doge's Palace by taking them through the maze of secret passageways and hidden chambers. It includes the seven prison cells beneath the lead roof, from one of which Casanova made his famous escape in 1755, as well as the torture chambers and the Doge's private apartments. There is a conducted tour in English daily starting at 10.30am: book on 041-522 4951, or at the kiosk in the palace courtyard.

The Sala del Maggior Consiglio

Map
on page
35

Bridge of Sighs
The Ponte dei Sospiri was named after the sighs of prisoners as they were led over the bridge to torture or execution – or so the story goes. In fact, by the time this bridge was built in the 17th century, the cells were comparatively civilised and used only to house petty offenders. Only one political prisoner ever crossed the bridge.

Prison interior

Republic in 1797. The ceiling and the long walls glorify Venetian victories. On the entrance wall is a magnificent *Last Judgement* by Palma il Giovane, and on the wall opposite a triumphal arch was erected in 1694 for Doge Morosini in honour of a victorious battle against the Turks; it contains allegorical paintings by Gregorio Lazzarini.

Z Sala della Quarantia Criminale. Nothing remains of this room apart from its gilt ceiling. The marble originals of *Adam and Eve* by Antonio Rizzo have now been placed here *(see page 32)*. The adjoining Sala del Magistrato alle Leggi 1 has a fine collection of Flemish art, notably Hieronymous Bosch's *Triptych of the Hermits* and *Paradise and Empyrean.*

From the Scala dei Censori [**T**] several narrow passageways lead across the ★★ **Ponte dei Sospiri** (Bridge of Sighs, immortalised in Lord Byron's *Childe Harold*) to the *prigioni nuove* (new prisons). The way out passes the Sala dei Censori, the Avogaria (room used by a branch of the judiciary) and the Cancelleria (study). The dark dungeons known as the *pozzi* (wells) are also in this section of the building, and were reserved for the most dangerous criminals.

COLOSSAL COLUMNS

We now come back out into the open air; a few steps to the right are the **Colonne di San Marco e San Teodoro** (Columns of St Mark and St Theodore). These colossal granite monoliths were brought to Venice from the Orient in the 12th century and have stood on the Molo since 1172. Between these two columns death sentences were passed, and many superstitious Venetians thus avoid walking through them. The lion of St Mark on the column on the palace side is of Oriental origin, and was once gilded. The statue of St Theodore on the other side (St Theodore was the patron saint of Venice before the relics of St Mark were acquired) is thought to be a Roman likeness of Mithradates, king of Pontus.

2: Canal Grande

Piazzale Roma – Ferrovia – Rialto – Accademia – San Marco

A trip along the S-shaped ★★★ **Canal Grande** (nearly 4km/2½ miles long), which divides the city into two halves, is an unforgettable experience. Wealthy merchants and noble families positioned the facades of their houses to face the water. The city's geographical situation – 4km (2½ miles) from the mainland and 2km (1¼ miles) from the open sea – meant that the island was strategically secure, so warehouses, shops and private homes could be built in an open manner.

The following is limited to a selection of the most important buildings to look out for during a *vaporetto* (water-bus) or gondola trip along the Canal Grande, from the railway station to St Mark's Square. *(See page 120 for details of vaporetti routes.)*

AROUND THE STATION

Opposite the station, the large green dome and the portico of the church of **San Simeone Piccolo** ❿ catch the eye. Built in 1718–38, this was modelled on the Pantheon in Rome. Today it is used as a concert hall.

On the station side, just before the first bridge,

Map on page 40

Star Attractions
● Bridge of Sighs
● Canal Grande

Below: gondoliers take a break
Bottom: La Salute view

the facade of **Santa Maria degli Scalzi** ⓫ comes into view, with its mighty twin columns on two storeys and extravagant sculpture. The church, a fine example of Venetian neoclassicism, was designed by Giuseppe Sardi and completed in 1689 *(see page 79)*. The bridge over the Canal Grande (one of only three) was built when Venice was first connected to the railway network in 1858; the former iron bridge was replaced by today's stone one in 1934.

CHURCHES AND PALACES

Opposite the Riva di Biagio landing-stage is the church of **San Geremia** ⓬. Unusually, because of its position right at the junction of the Cannaregio Canal and the Canal Grande, this church was provided with two facades. Just beyond the church on the Cannaregio Canal is the **Palazzo Labia** (1750), a monumental neoclassical structure

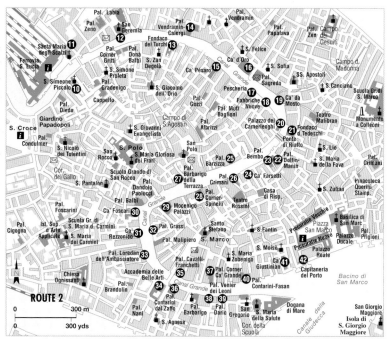

which was built by a wealthy family of merchants from Catalonia *(see page 79)*.

The next landing-stage is named after the church beside it, **San Marcuola**. Its brick facade only appears archaic – it was in fact constructed in the 18th century and never completed.

Across the canal stands what used to be one of the finest Veneto-Byzantine buildings in the city until it was unfeelingly restored in the 19th century, the **Fondaco dei Turchi** ⑬, which today houses the Museo di Storia Naturale (Natural History Museum). This, the largest palazzo on the Canal Grande, dates from the 13th century and used to belong to the dukes of Ferrara; the Republic used to 'borrow' the palace for state ceremonies. From 1621 to 1838 it was the warehouse of Turkish merchants. The museum, reopened after renovation to the building, includes a dinosaur skeleton some 110 million years old.

The 15th -century brick building next door with the lion of St Mark on the wall used to house the *depositi del megio* (the granaries of the Republic). Opposite it is the ★ **Palazzo Vendramin-Calergi** ⑭, a massive Renaissance building by Mauro Codussi. The double-mullioned windows inside a large arch with a circle is a feature borrowed from Tuscany. Richard Wagner died here in 1883 while a guest of the Duke of Chambord. The palazzo is the winter home of the Casino.

CA' PESARO

The next landing-stage is called San Stae *(see page 64.)* Next along this bank comes the ★★ **Ca' Pésaro** ⑮, built by Baldassare Longhena (1598–1682), whose monumental facades are a distinctive feature of the city. The most interesting aspect of this building, a superb example of Venetian baroque, is the structural combination of sculpture decoration and columns – a recipe first used in Venice by Jacopo Sansovino when he built the Old Library *(see page 19)*. Begun in 1676, the Ca' Pésaro was only completed by Antonio Gaspari in 1710. Today it houses the Gallery of Modern Art and the Oriental Museum *(see page 64)*.

Star Attraction
● Ca' Pésaro

What's in a name?
Until the end of the 17th century the Doge's Palace was the only building in Venice allowed to be called a palazzo. Other splendid mansions were called simply Casa (house), shortened to Ca'. Many families did not bother to rename their houses *palazzi* once it was permitted, hence Ca' d'Oro, Ca' da Mosto and so on.

Opposite: the Scalzi Bridge
Below: Ca' Pésaro

Map on page 40

CA' D'ORO

The next landing-stage is named after Venice's most magnificent Gothic palace, the ★★ **Ca' d'Oro** ⓰, built between 1421 and 1440. Its name ('Golden House') derives from its facade, which was formerly gilded. The first loggia floor features the same decorative motifs as the facade of the Doge's Palace, here exercising its influence a full 100 years later. The round arches in the middle of the ground floor presage the Renaissance. However magnificent the palace may look today, it was actually never completed; the left extension of the right wing was never built. The interior of the Ca' d'Oro has been restored and is a gallery of paintings and sculpture *(see page 83)*.

Below: the Pescheria
Bottom: the Ca' d'Oro

MARKET HALLS

This fine Gothic jewel is followed by a neo-Gothic building, the **Pescheria** ⓱, a hall built in 1907 to house the fish market. On the same side, adjoining the **Erberia** (wholesale market for fruit and vegetables), is the long arcaded **Fabbriche Nuove** ⓲. In 1513 a fire destroyed the Rialto quarter, and everything had to be rebuilt; this early example of Renaissance architecture is the work of Jacopo Sansovino (1552–55). Right at the centre of the 25 arches facing the water, take a look across at the 13th-century ★ **Ca' da Mosto** ⓳ on the other

bank, a good example of the Veneto-Byzantine style. From the 16th to the 18th century, this building was the Leon Bianco Inn, Venice's leading hotel, whose guests included Emperor Joseph II and the painter J.M.W. Turner.

The Canal Grande now begins its sharp curve to the right that leads to the Rialto Bridge. On the right before the bridge is the **Palazzo dei Camerlenghi** ⑳, which also had to be rebuilt after the fire of 1513. Directly opposite is the facade of the **Fondaco (Fontego) dei Tedeschi** ㉑, the former trading centre of the German merchants *(see page 53)*. Today it houses the central Post Office. The building was reconstructed in 1505 by Spavento and completed by Scarpagnino.

AROUND THE RIALTO

Until around 150 years ago, the **Rialto Bridge** *(see page 59)* was the only way of crossing the canal on foot. This is the heart of Venice, the commercial centre where the Republic began to flourish.

The **Palazzo Dolfin-Manin** ㉒ on the west bank houses a modern commercial centre, the Banca d'Italia. Its white Renaissance facade, by Sansovino (1538), harmonises well with its blue awnings. Next door, in sharp contrast, is the **Palazzo Bembo** ㉓, with a Venetian Gothic facade.

Among the row of seven houses that now follow it's worth keeping an eye out for a narrow white house situated roughly at their centre; its windows have Moorish pointed arches.

Next on the same side is another magnificent Byzantine building, the **Ca' Farsetti** ㉔. Its arches are no longer functional, but are a decorative principle in their own right, covering the entire facade. Ca' Farsetti, built by Doge Enrico Dandolo, was heavily restored in the 19th century, and today houses the *municipio* (town hall).

Across the canal, next to the San Silvestro landing-stage, stands the red **Palazzo Barzizza** ㉕, a rare example of a Byzantine house (12th- to 13th-century). The remarkable reliefs on its facade date from the time it was built. Back on the left side is the colossal facade of the **Palazzo Grimani** ㉖,

Star Attraction
● Ca' d'Oro

Venetian adventurer
The explorer Alvise da Mosto (1432–1483, also known as Cadamosto, after his home) was born in Ca' da Mosto. In the employ of Portuguese king Henry the Navigator, he explored the coast of West Africa as far as modern Guinea-Bissau, and wrote one of the first accounts of the region. He was probably the first European to reach the Cape Verde islands, which he 'discovered' in 1456.

An evening gondola ride

Map
on page
40

Palazzo poet

Lord Byron lived mainly in Venice between 1816 and 1819. He wrote much of his best work in Italy and, while staying at the Palazzo Mocenigo, began his longest, wittiest and most insightful poem, *Don Juan*. It was not unknown for him to swim from the Lido back to his lodgings at the Palazzo.

*Below: a Mocenigo balcony
Bottom: water markers*

a mighty Renaissance building by Michele Sanmicheli of Verona (early 16th-century). Next to it is the elegant Late Gothic loggia of the Palazzo Corner Contarini dei Cavalli (15th-century).

The right bank provides a good opportunity to study the different architectural styles: there is a colourful row of facades with Byzantine, Gothic and Renaissance arches. A particularly fine Late Gothic building is the ★ **Palazzo Barbarigo della Terrazza** ㉗, built around 1442, with its distinctive balconied terrace.

To the left of the Sant' Angelo landing-stage is the superb Early Renaissance ★ **Palazzo Corner-Spinelli** ㉘, built by Mauro Codussi at the end of the 15th century, with its rusticated ground floor and attractive balconies. Opposite the San Tomà landing-stage stand the four **Mocenigo Palazzi** ㉙; the first one, a Renaissance building, has blue awnings that liven up its facade. Lord Byron's lodgings were in the second one, which is rather wider and not quite as spectacular; the building has lions' heads along its full length.

CANAL BEND

At the bend in the Canal Grande here, the Rio di Ca' Foscari joins it from the right; on the other side of this junction is the complex making up the ★ **Ca' Foscari** ㉚, now the University of Venice.

It is one of the last Late Gothic structures in the city, with four storeys rather than the more usual three. Doge Foscari (1423–57) had the previous building demolished in 1452 and then rebuilt in its present form. It has fine tracery, and a frieze of putti bearing the Foscari arms.

*Below: Palazzo
Corner-Spinelli
Bottom: Ca' Rezzonico*

The monumental neoclassical ★ **Ca' Rezzonico ㉛**, on the right of the landing-stage of the same name, was built by Baldassare Longhena in the middle of the 17th century. Its fine 18th-century interior decoration has been preserved.

Directly opposite is the **Palazzo Grassi ㉜**, designed by Giorgio Massari and considered the most remarkable example of 18th-century neoclassicism in the city. To the right of it is the 12th-century campanile of the former church of San Samuele, one of the oldest bell-towers in Venice.

The Palazzo Grassi was bought by Fiat in 1984 and elegantly restored and renovated by Antonio Foscari and Musée d'Orsay architect Gae Aulenti. It is now a cultural centre (open: daily 10am–7pm, tel: 041-523 1680), staging exhibitions.

On the right bank once again, we now pass a Late Gothic building, the 15th-century **Palazzo Loredan dell'Ambasciatore ㉝**, with Lombard-esque Early Renaissance sculptures in its niches. The building was the Austrian embassy in the 18th century.

PONTE DELL'ACCADEMIA

Beside the **Ponte dell'Accademia** is the tall, narrow-shouldered façade of the former church of Santa Maria della Carità. At right-angles to it is the façade of the **Accademia delle Belle Arte ㉞**, built by Giorgio Massari (1760), which today houses one of the most important collections of paintings in Venice (*see page 77*).

Just after the bridge, on the left bank, stands the ★ **Palazzo Cavalli-Franchetti ㉟**; its artistic 15th-century windows were inspired by those of the Doge's Palace. The second building after the bridge on the right is the long ★ **Palazzo Contarini dal Zaffo ㊱**, one of the finest examples of late 15th-century Lombardesque architecture in Venice.

Map on page 40

Popular Palace
Author and art critic John Ruskin and his wife Effie rented a suite of rooms in the Gritti Palace Hotel in 1851, when he was working on the last two volumes of his influential work *The Stones of Venice*. It was also Ernest Hemingway's favourite hotel in the city.

Opposite is the **Palazzo Corner Ca' Grande** ❸, designed by Sansovino in 1532. His innovations included the rusticated ground floor and the triple-arched entrance. The upper storeys are lent emphasis by the use of Ionic columns on the first floor and Corinthian on the second. Today the building is used by the provincial administration and the Prefecture.

On the right bank directly opposite is a one-storey flat-roofed building with a garden in front, the **Palazzo Venier dei Leoni** ❸. Dating from 1749, it now houses the Peggy Guggenheim Collection of Modern Art *(see page 77)*. The Biennale has organised an international architectural competition for the building's completion.

THREE PALAZZI

On the same side there is another Early Renaissance jewel, the ★ **Palazzo Dario** ❸. This Lombardesque building, with its polychromatic marble intarsias, was built in the late 15th century, possibly by Pietro Lombardo himself.

On the other side of the canal, the 15th-century **Palazzo Pisani-Gritti** is easy to spot; today it is the celebrated Gritti Palace Hotel. A side-canal now joins the Canal Grande, and the third house beyond it is the tiny, delightful ★ **Palazzo Contarini-Fasan** ❹. It has wheel tracery on its balcony, and is traditionally called 'The House of Desdemona', after a Venetian lady reputedly the model for Shakespeare's heroine in *Othello*.

Palazzo Dario

ANCIENT OFFICES

Among the hotels that line the canal near St Mark's, the only really striking-looking building is the **Ca' Giustinian** ❹, a Late Gothic structure *(circa* 1474), today housing the headquarters of the Venice Biennale and the administrative offices of the Venice Tourist Office. To the right of the San Marco landing-stage is the **Capitaneria del Porto** ❹, a late-15th-century Lombardesque building. From 1756 to 1807 it was the headquarters of the Accademia di Pittura e di Scultura (chaired by Tiepolo); today it is the Port Authority Office.

3: Three Sestieri

San Marco – Campo Sant'Angelo – Campo San Luca – Campo San Bartolomeo – San Giovanni Crisostomo – Santi Apostoli – Santa Maria dei Miracoli – Santi Giovanni e Paolo

Map on page 48

The centre of Venice is divided in to six sections called *sestieri* (sixths). This route explores three of them in a relatively compact area around St Mark's Square: Sestiere San Marco to the west of the basilica, Sestiere Castello to the east, and part of Sestiere Cannaregio, to the north.

From the west end of the Piazza San Marco, the Salizzada San Moisè leads to the church of the same name, and the Calle del Ridotto branches off in front of it. *Ridotto* formerly meant 'club' (redoubt or hideaway), and so much gambling took place in this part of the city that the municipal authorities closed down many establishments in 1774. Today this street contains the entrance to the **Ca' Giustinian** *(see page 46)*.

Below: San Moisè facade
Bottom: Campo Santa Maria Nova

SAN MOISE

The church of **San Moisè** ❸ dates from the 8th century, and received its present appearance in 1688. Its over-elaborate facade has several sculptures by Arrigo Merengo (the Austrian Heinrich Meyring), who also designed the high altar. After

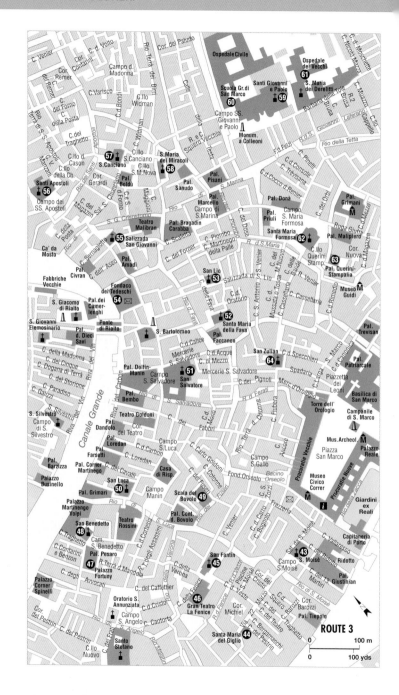

Map on page 48

the bridge comes the Calle Larga 22 Marzo, commemorating the day in 1848 when the Austrian occupiers were chased out of the city (but for only one year).

Crossing a canal, the street emerges at the square in front of the church of **Santa Maria del Giglio** ⓴, called *Zobenigo* by the Venetians after the Jubanico family who founded the previous building on the site in the 9th century. The overladen baroque facade by Sardi (1678–81) was financed by the Barbaro family. The facade bears portraits of them and plans of Crete, Padua, Rome, Corfu and so on, recording the victories of various family members. Beneath the organ in the sanctuary is a work by Tintoretto of the Evangelists. The *Madonna and Child with the Young St John* in the sacristy is actually half a Rubens: the central section is genuine, the rest painted by someone else.

CAMPO SAN FANTIN

Halfway back to San Moisè, the sign to Teatro La Fenice leads to the Campo San Fantin. The small church of **San Fantin** ㊺ seems very inconspicuous at first, even though it was built by two famous architects, Scarpagnino and Sansovino, who began it in 1507 and completed it in 1564. Opposite the church stood the **Gran Teatro La Fenice** ㊻, until the catastrophic fire of 1996.

The small, two-storeyed palazzo with the triangular gable opposite the church is today known as the Ateneo Veneto and is a concert and conference centre. When it was built at the end of the 16th century it was the Scuola di San Girolamo, whose members used to console condemned prisoners before their execution.

The Calle della Fenice leads as far as a covered arcade and a bridge. At the next right fork the Calle Caotorta comes out into the **Campo Sant'Angelo** (**Anzolo**). The leaning campanile of the former convent of Santo Stefano can be seen to the left; the plain wall along the canal here hides a superb Renaissance cloister that can be admired during office hours (the building is used by the financial administration).

Fire and the Fenice

In 1774 Venice's leading opera house, the San Benedetto Theatre, was burnt to the ground. In its place, a phoenix rose from the ashes – La Fenice, on Campo San Fantin, which opened to a rapturous public in 1792. The new theatre, which had been ravaged by fire during its construction, burnt down again in 1836. But it rose once more and reopened in December 1837. Many of Verdi's operas had their first performance here. Most recently, on 29 January 1996, fire destroyed the ill-fated Fenice for a third time. The restoration has been delayed by accusations of corruption in assigning building contracts and there is no telling when this phoenix will rise again. Meanwhile, opera-lovers can watch performances in the temporary auditorium of the PalaFenice at Tronchetto *(see page 112)*.

Campo Sant'Angelo angel

Map on page 48

FORTUNY COLLECTION

Leave the campo via Calle della Mandola, a busy shopping street, and the first turn-off to the left, the Rio Terrà della Mandola, leads to the **Palazzo Fortuny ❹** (formerly the Palazzo Pesaro), home of the Fortuny Collection. This displays the artistic and scientific achievements of Mariano Fortuny y Madrazo (1871–1949), a Spanish-born 'Renaissance Man' *(see box, left)*. The 15th-century Gothic facade is impressive, as is the carefully preserved ★ **interior courtyard** with its fine old wooden staircase. Most of the palazzo is closed for restoration but you can visit the exhibition of Fortuny's paintings, fabrics, costumes and photographs (open: Tues–Sun, 10am–5pm).

One side of the building dominates the campo and the church of **San Benedetto (Beneto) ❹**, which contains Tiepolo's *San Francesco di Paola* (18th-century) in the first side-altar to the left.

Silk master

Mariano Fortuny took over the Palazzo Pesaro in 1899, renamed it after himself and lived there until his death in 1949. He patented his famous pleated silk process in 1899, a technique by which hand-made pleats are set into moistened material before being sewn into place, then sealed by heat.

Fortuny loved to work with rich fabrics and natural colours, drawing on Renaissance and Oriental inspirations for his stencilled patterns. The fabric is still made on the Giudecca – and sold for very high prices. Fortuny lamps are exquisite works of art, covered with silk and trimmed with Murano glass beads.

Palazzo Fortuny courtyard

SCALA DEL BOVOLO

The Salizzada del Teatro leads back to the Calle della Mandola. Turn left into the Campo Manin with its mighty **monument** (1875) to Daniele Manin, who led the revolution against the Austrian occupation (1848–49). Follow the yellow sign suspended at the entrance of the narrow alley to the right of the monument, which points to the ★★ **Scala del Bovolo ❹**. This is the beautiful external spiral staircase of the Palazzo Contarini (*bovolo* means 'snail' in Venetian dialect), an astounding Lombardesque work dating from 1499.

Cross this square now, and turn left at the modern Cassa di Risparmio to reach the campo containing the church of **San Luca ❺**. The high altarpiece here of *The Virgin Appearing to St Luke* is by Paolo Veronese (16th-century).

Retrace your steps to the Cassa Risparmio and turn left into the Campo San Luca, a popular rendezvous-point for Venetians. A carved stone post with a flagpole marks the historic centre of Venice. Next to the Teatro Goldoni, Calle San Luca opens out on to the Calle dei Fabbri.

Cross the bridge to the right (Ponte dell'Ovo),

which leads to the church of **San Salvatore (San Salvador)** 🜸 (open: daily 9am–noon and 4–7pm), built between 1506 and 1534 by architects Spavento, Tullio, Pietro Lombardo and Sansovino. The lateral portal in the Lombardesque style dates from that time; the facade was reworked and given sculptures by Sardi in 1663.

The ★★**interior** is a superb example of Venetian High Renaissance architecture: clear lines, a generous three-aisled basilica with three domes, and cleverly arranged pillars along the nave. The most eye-catching works of art here are not necessarily the most valuable: there are two sculptures by Sansovino, *Carità* (Charity) and *Speranza* (Hope), next to the tomb of Doge Francesco Venier. The third altar on the right contains Titian's *Annunciation*, painted in 1566. The main altar contains a silver reredos, a masterpiece by Venetian silversmiths (1290) that is revealed only between 3 and 15 August every year. This is compensated for by the fact that it is covered by a fine Titian *(Transfigurazione).*

GUILD HEADQUARTERS

When you leave the church through the main door, the **Scuola Grande di San Teodoro** (built 1579–1648) is hard to miss. St Theodore was Venice's patron saint before the city acquired the

Star Attractions
● Scala del Bovolo
● San Salvatore interior

*Below: Scala del Bovolo
Bottom: the nave of
San Salvatore*

relics of St Mark. This *scuola (see page 10)* was devoted to merchants and arts and crafts, and the wares on sale on the ground floor reflect this. The building is now used for concerts and exhibitions.

From the Marzarieta 2 Aprile the route continues down the first street to the right, the Calle degli Stagneri, over a bridge to the church of **Santa Maria della Fava** ❺❷, with its archaic-looking brick facade; the building actually dates from the 18th century. The interior is neoclassical and harmonious (Antonio Gaspari, 1711). The combination of light and dark provides a fine setting for two remarkable paintings: a Tiepolo in the first altar to the right and a Piazzetta in the second altar to the left (18th-century).

Below: Goldoni's statue
Bottom: the Fondaco dei Tedeschi

FONDACO DEI TEDESCHI

On the left-hand side of the church, the Calle della Fava branches off and ends up at the Campo San Lio. **San Lio church** ❺❸ is worth visiting for a look at its *James the Apostle* by Titian (on the left-hand wall of the second altar).

The continuation of the Salizzada San Lio (in the opposite direction from the church) leads to the Ponte Sant'Antonio; the ensuing shopping arcade then ends at the Campo San Bartolomeo, one of the busiest squares in the city, with its monument to the playwright Goldoni (1883). The **Fondaco**

(Fontego) dei Tedeschi (54), right next to the Rialto Bridge, was once the German merchants' trading centre and today houses the central Post Office. The present Renaissance building by Giorgio Spavento and Sansovino (1505–8) has some fine arcades in its ★ **interior courtyard**, which has a graceful, almost playful atmosphere to it.

SAN GIOVANNI CRISOSTOMO

Beyond the bridge, the Salizzada San Giovanni Crisostomo leads to the Renaissance **San Giovanni Crisostomo church** (55), the last work of Mauro Codussi (1497–1504), who loved curved facades. The spatial relationships within have been somewhat disturbed by over-ornate decoration, though three works should definitely be mentioned: the chiaroscuro over the high altar by Sebastiano del Piombo (1509–11) is very hard to see; Giovanni Bellini's *Saints Christopher, Jerome and Louis of Toulouse* (1513), one of his last works, is more visible, in the first side-altar to the right; and directly opposite, on the left-hand wall, the marble altar by Tullio Lombardo (1500–2) has a classical bas-relief of the *Coronation of the Virgin*.

SANTI APOSTOLI

The Salizzada San Giovanni Crisostomo now leads over a bridge where the Salizzada San Canciano branches off to the right. Across Campizello Corner, to the left, is a covered arcade with a bridge leading to the campo and church of ★ **Santi Apostoli** (56), which underwent all kinds of aesthetically unsuccessful exterior alterations until the middle of the 18th century. The Cappella Corner (15th-century) by Mauro Codussi, an elegant Early Renaissance domed chapel, still survives; the altar has a *Communion of St Lucia* by Tiepolo (18th-century). The church's campanile is one of Venice's tallest.

From the square in front of the church the route now continues across the Campiello Cason and over the canal to the church of **San Canciano** (57), which was given its quiet pilastered facade by

Marco the Millionaire

On the right of San Giovanni Crisostomo are two interconnecting courtyards known as the Corte del Milion. Marco Polo is said to have lived in the Corte Seconda until his death in 1324. *Il Milione* (*The Million*), the title of the book he dictated while in prison, refers to the vast number of extraordinary sights and adventures he recalled from his travels. Eventually, the name came to be associated with the courtyard where the Polo family house was supposedly located.

Santi Apostoli clock and bell tower

Map on page 48

Antonio Gaspari in 1705. From here the bridge is only a few steps away to the left: boats used to leave for Murano from this part of the bank in former days.

Members of the Chorus

Santa Maria dei Miracoli is just one of Venice's major churches that can be visited on one 15,000-lire ticket (entrance to each church individually costs 3,000 lire). The others covered by the 'Chorus' pass are: Santo Stefano, Santa Maria Gloriosa dei Frari, Santa Maria del Giglio, Santa Maria Formosa (currently under restoration), San Polo, San Giacomo dell'Orio, San Stae, Sant'Alvise, San Sebastiano (currently closed on Sundays), San Pietro di Castello Redentore and La Madonna dell'Orto. You can buy a Chorus pass at any of these churches. Opening hours are usually 10am–5pm Monday to Saturday, 1–6pm Sunday.

SANTA MARIA DEI MIRACOLI

A few steps in the opposite direction and straight across the square is the church of ★ **Santa Maria dei Miracoli 😵** (open: Mon–Sat 10am–5pm, Sun 1–5pm). To Venetians accustomed to brick facades, the Lombardesque style of this church, which was built by the Lombardo family of architects between 1481 and 1489, must have looked extremely odd. Fine polychrome marble inlay is the only form of decoration here, and Late Gothic formal geometry is reduced to a series of semi-circles and right-angles: Tuscan architecture had finally arrived in Venice.

The interior of the church is surprisingly simple, with just one aisle, and the smooth walls are broken up only by the marble decoration. The vaulted and coffered ceiling, by Pier Maria Pennacchi and helpers (1528) contains 50 different portraits of prophets and patriarchs. The raised choir is particularly fine, with superb marble inlay work on the triumphal arch, exquisite carving, and an eye-catching polychrome marble cross, typical of the Lombardesque style. The

Santa Maria dei Miracoli

Madonna at the altar is said to work miracles, and was the original reason for the construction of this Renaissance jewel.

SAN ZANIPOLO

The Calle Larga Gallina leads around the apse and then to the right across the bridge to the ★★ **Campo di Santi Giovanni e Paolo**, one of the most impressive-looking squares in the city. It contains the broad Gothic brick facade of the church of Santi Giovanni e Paolo; right next to it, at right angles, is the former Scuola Grande di San Marco with its cheerful semicircular facade, so typical of the Early Renaissance; and looking down rather gruffly at all this, the *condottiero* (commander of mercenaries), Bartolomeo Colleoni, whose huge ★★ **equestrian statue** stands prominently in the square.

*Below: the Colleoni equestrian statue
Bottom: Santi Giovanni e Paolo stained glass*

Colleoni was a mercenary from Bergamo who, shortly before his death in 1475, left a legacy to the Republic on condition that an equestrian monument was erected in his honour in the Piazza San Marco. In 1479 the Signoria ordered that it should be erected in front of the Scuola di San Marco instead. The Florentine sculptor Verrocchio received the commission for the statue, and it was finished after his death by Alessandro Leopardi, who also did the pedestal. Ever since its official unveiling in 1496, 'the Colleoni' has been considered one of the world's finest equestrian statues.

The Dominican church of ★★ **Santi Giovanni e Paolo** ⑳ (open: Mon–Sat 8am–12.30pm and 3.30–6pm, Sun 3–6pm), familiar to Venetians as *San Zanipolo*, was started in 1234 and completed 200 years later in the Gothic style of mendicant order churches. Together with the Frari, this is Venice's finest Gothic church. The upper section of the facade is harmonious; the lower section seems never to have been fully completed. The centre portal by Bartolomeo Bon (1464), however, is a masterpiece of Late Gothic sculpture; the bas-reliefs of the *Annunciation* flanking it are 13th-century Byzantine. The interior is divided by mighty columns of Istrian stone

Maps
on pages
48 & 57

blocks, connected by wooden tie-beams, in three vaulted aisles; the main apse and the high altar are each flanked by two choir chapels. San Zanipolo is the burial-place of no less than 25 doges.

SAN ZANIPOLO'S TREASURES

A Tomb of Doge Giovanni Mocenigo, *circa* 1500, by Tullio Lombardo.

B Tomb of Doge Pietro Mocenigo, completed in 1481 by Pietro Lombardo.

C Polyptych of St Vincent Ferrer, Dominican monk. These nine panels by Giovanni Bellini (1464) are an Early Renaissance masterpiece.

D Chapel of St Dominic, added between 1690 and 1716. Ceiling painting of the *Saint in Glory* by Giovanni Battista Piazzetta (1727).

E On the wall, *Christ Bearing the Cross* by Alvise Vivarini (late 15th-century). Stained glass of the window (late 15th-century) was made in Murano. Also includes *The Alms-giving of St Anthony* by Lorenzo Lotto (1542).

F **Choir**. On the right-hand wall, tomb of Doge Michele Morosini (died 1382), contemporary Gothic; beyond it, tomb of Leonardo Loredan (1572). On the left-hand wall, tomb of Doge Marco Corner (1365–68, the oldest in the church); behind it, tomb of Doge Andrea Vendramin (1476–78) by Tullio Lombardo

Below: the tomb of Pietro Mocenigo
Bottom: the St Dominic ceiling

(*circa* 1492), the finest of all the doge tombs.

G Chapel of the Rosary, added in 1582. Both rooms contain important works by Paolo Veronese (16th-century).

H Tomb of Doge Pasquale Malipiero (1457–1462) by Pietro Lombardo.

I Tomb of Doge Tommaso Mocenigo (1414–23), with an innovative baldachin carved out of stone, otherwise Gothic. Next to it (in line with the pillar) the tomb of Doge Niccolò Marcello (1473–74) by Pietro Lombardo, completed in 1481.

J Renaissance altar with good copy of a masterpiece by Titian, *St Peter Martyr* (1530).

ANOTHER SCUOLA GRANDE

At right-angles to the church facade stands the ★**Scuola Grande di San Marco** 60, formerly a goldsmiths' and silk merchants' philanthropic confraternity, and today the civic hospital. The *trompe l'oeil* panels on the two-storeyed facade are very noticeable; the lions appear almost three-dimensional. The facade was designed by the Lombardo family, and finished by Mauro Codussi.

From here it is just a few steps to the monumental facade of the ★**Ospedaletto** 61 (or Santa Maria del Riposo), rebuilt by Baldassare Longhena in 1674. It is possible to visit the Sala della Musica with its 18th-century frescoes and a small display of old musical instruments (Thursday to Saturday, April to September 4–7pm, October to March 3–6pm).

SANTA MARIA FORMOSA

The Calle dell'Ospedaletto leads to the Calle Lunga Santa Maria Formosa, at the end of which is the Campo Santa Maria Formosa. The church of **Santa Maria Formosa** 62 (currently closed for restoration) was probably founded in the 7th century. It assumed its present form in 1492, and its interior is one of many to

> **The Numbers Game**
> Venice may have invented the idea of address numbers, and the curious ancient system is still in use. Each of the 'sixths' *(sestieri)* of the city has one No 1, then the ensuing numbers wind up and down the streets and alleys with no apparent pattern. The Doge's Palace is No 1 San Marco and near the main post office there is a large sign proclaiming '5562: The Last Number of the Sestiere San Marco'. To find addresses, Venetians use the *Indicatore Anagrafico*, a book that matches numbers to streets.

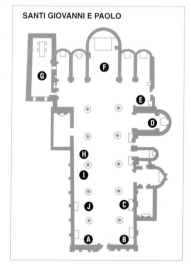

SANTI GIOVANNI E PAOLO

Map on page 48

Below: Campiello Querini
Bottom: Gothic arch,
Calle del Paradiso

have been based on a Greek cross, like San Marco. Mauro Codussi put an Early Renaissance facade on the side facing the campo in 1604.

The route continues right round the church to reach the small street leading to the delightful ★ **Campiello Querini**. Three canals meet here, and the various bridges afford magnificent views.

The ★ **Palazzo Querini-Stampalia** ⑬ (open: daily 10am–1pm and 3–6pm; extended to 10pm Fri and Sat in summer), a 16th-century building, was the residence of the patriarchs of Venice from 1807 to 1850. It contains an impressive collection of paintings by Giovanni Bellini, Palma Giovane, Palma Vecchio, Pietro Longhi, Tiepolo and others, as well as the unusual series of 69 paintings by Gabriele Bella (mid-18th century) illustrating *Scene di vita pubblica veneziana* (Scenes of Public Life in Venice).

CALLE DEL PARADISO

Along the canal that passes to the side of the church of Santa Maria Formosa, the second bridge leads across to the **Calle del Paradiso**; a Gothic pointed arch made of marble, with a Madonna, can be seen between the houses at the entrance to the street. The houses here are ancient, some of them dating from the 13th century, and this antiquity is what gives the Calle del Paradiso its special flair: both rows of houses have projecting first floors with charming medieval timberwork.

At the end of the Calle del Paradiso, the Salizzada San Lio leads off left to the Calle delle Bande. Turn right here, cross over a bridge and you reach the back of the church of San Giuliano, known to the Venetians as **San Zulian** ⑭. The facade is by Sansovino (1553–5). The church was commissioned by Tommaso Rangone, a doctor from Ravenna, and as well as his bronze statue (also by Sansovino) there are several inscriptions in Greek and Hebrew along the walls.

Near the back of the church, on the right, the Calle degli Specchieri begins. It was originally the street of mirror-makers (an offshoot of the city's glassmaking industry).

4: West of the Rialto

Rialto – Campo San Polo – Ca' Pésaro – San Giacomo dell'Orio – the Frari – Scuola Grande di San Rocco – Ca' Rezzonico

The Sestiere San Polo still bears evidence of the days when it was the city's trading centre – quaysides, busy shops and vibrant markets. To the south of the area, around the Campo dei Frari, are some of Venice's most beautiful religious and secular buildings.

The ★★ **Rialto Bridge** ❻❺ crosses the Canal Grande at the heart of what used to be the busiest trading centre in the city. The names of the quays reflect it: the Fondamenta del Vino (wine) lies opposite the Fondamenta del Carbon (charcoal) and Fondamenta del Ferro (iron). Fruit and vegetables are still traded at the Rialto. Today's stone bridge, 48m (157ft) long, was completed in 1591.

COMMERCIAL QUARTER

Directly to the right of the bridge, on the canal bank, stands the Palazzo dei Camerlenghi, a Renaissance building (1525–28, built after the fire of 1513). It used to be a financial administration building, and debtors were imprisoned behind the barred windows of its basement floor.

The bridge leads into the Ruga degli Orefici

Map on page 60

Star Attraction
● Rialto Bridge

Winning design
The Republic held a competition for the design of the first stone bridge across the Canal Grande (there had been three earlier wooden bridges). Among those who submitted entries were Michelangelo and Palladio (who proposed a bridge covered in temples and statues). The prize went to the relatively unknown – and aptly named – Antonio da Ponte. His design echoed the sharply sloping shape of the previous wooden bridge, adding the slanting arcades that still contain shops today.

The Rialto

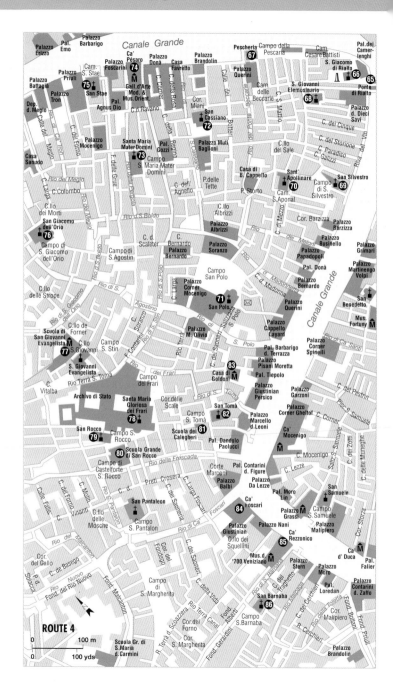

Canale Grande

Palazzo Erizzo
Pal. Emo
Palazzo Barbarigo
Ca' Pésaro
Palazzo Donà
Casa Favretto
Palazzo Brandolin
Pescheria
Campo della Pescaria
Cam. Cesare Battisti
Pal. dei Camer- lenghi

Palazzo Foscarini
74
Cam. S. Stae
Palazzo Querini
S. Giacomo di Rialto
66
65

Palazzo Priuli
Palazzo Tron
75
Gall.d'Arte Mod. & Mus.Orient.
Cam. delle Beccarie
S. Giovanni Elemosinario
68
Ponte di Rialto

Palazzo Battagia
San Stae
Pal. Agnus Dio
C. d. Ravano
Cor. Miani
C. S. Matteo
C. del Storione

Dep. d. Megio
San Cassiano
72
Palazzo Muti Baglioni
C.llo del Sale
C. dei Cinque

Casa Sanudo
Palazzo Mocenigo
Santa Maria Mater Domini
73
Campo S. Maria Mater Domini
Pal. Regina Gozzi
C. dell'Agnello
P.delle Tette
Casa di B. Cappello
Sant' Apollinare
70
C. Paradiso
San Silvestro
69

C.llo dei Morti
C.llo Albrizzi
P. Storto
Cam. S.Aponal
Campo di S. Silvestro
Cor. Barzizza
Palazzo Barzizza

San Giacomo dell'Orio
76
Campo di S. Giacomo dell'Orio
Campo di S.Agostin
C. d. Scaleter
C. Bernardo
Palazzo Albrizzi
Palazzo Soranzo
Palazzo Businello
Palazzo Grimani

C.llo delle Strope
Rio di S.
Palazzo Bernardo
Campo San Polo
Palazzo Corner Mocenigo
71
San Polo
Palazzo Papadopoli
Pal. Donà
Palazzo Bernardo
Palazzo Querini
Palazzo Martinengo Volpi
San Benedetto

Scuola di San Giovanni Evangelista
77
C.llo de Forner
S. Giovanni Evangelista
Campo S. Stin
Palazzo M. Olivio
S. Polo
Palazzo Cappello Layard
Palazzo Corner Spinelli
Mus. Fortuny

C. Vitalba
Rio Terra S. Tomà
Campo dei Frari
Casa di Goldoni
83
Pal. Barbarigo d. Terrazza
Palazzo Pisani Moretta
Pal. Tiepolo
Palazzo Giustinian Persico
Palazzo Garzoni
C. dei Pestrin

Archivio di Stato
Santa Maria Gloriosa dei Frari
78
Cor.delle Scale
San Tomà
82
Palazzo Marcello d. Leoni
Palazzo Corner Gheltof
C. Corner

San Rocco
79
Campo S. Rocco
Scuola dei Caleghen
81
Pal. Dandolo Paolucci
Ca' Mocenigo

Scuola Grande di San Rocco
80
Campo di Castelforte S. Rocco
Rio della Frescada
Corte Marcani
Pal. Contarini d. Figure
Palazzo Balbi
Palazzo Da Lezze
C. Lezze
C. Mocenigo

Calle Falier
C.llo del Forno
Preti Crosera
San Pantaleon
Campo S. Pantalon
Pal. Moro Lin
Ca' Foscari
84
Palazzo Grassi
San Samuele
Campo S. Samuele
Palazzo Malipiero

Cor. del Gallo
C.llo delle Mosche
Rio del
Palazzo Giustinian
C.llo dei Squellini
Ca' Rezzonico
85
Ca' d' Duca
Pal. Falier

Fond. del Rio Nuovo
Campo di S. Margherita
Mus.d. '700 Veniziano
Palazzo Stern
Palazzo Moro
Pal. Loredan
Palazzo Contarini d. Zaffo

ROUTE 4

0 ___ 100 m
0 ___ 100 yds

Scuola Gr. di S.Maria d.Carmini
Cor del Forno
Cor. S. Margherita
Campo S. Barnaba
San Barnaba
86
Palazzo Brandolin
Cor. Malipiero

Map on page 60

(Oresi), or Goldsmiths Street. Today this shopping street provides all manner of inexpensive souvenirs. The goldsmiths still have a church consecrated to their patron saint: **San Giacomo di Rialto** ⑥⑥ (also known as San Giacometto), which was founded in 421 and is believed to be the oldest church in Venice. It is the only one still to possess a Gothic entrance portico. The most distinctive feature of the facade is the Gothic 24-hour clock dating from 1410; it was restored in the 17th century along with the rest of the building. Around the external apse is an inscription demanding honesty among the goldsmiths: 'Around This Temple Let the Merchant's Law Be Just, His Weight True, and His Covenants Faithful'.

CAMPO DI RIALTO

The Campo di Rialto in front of the church is enclosed by arcades built by Scarpagnino after the fire of 1513. The various laws of the Republic were proclaimed from the staircase opposite the church. The architectural impression of this square as a whole is unfortunately marred by all the market stalls and barrows.

The Ruga degli Orefici comes out into a small square with the market off to the right. Pass through the arcaded passageway to the bank of the Canal Grande,and the Byzantine Ca' da Mosto *(see page 42)* comes into view on the other bank. The picturesque wholesale market for fruit and vegetables, known as the ★★ **Erberia**, is held here each morning on the square next to the canal. The Calle delle Beccarie leads past the graceful neo-Gothic market hall housing the ★ **Pescheria** ⑥⑦ (fish market) to the Campo delle Beccarie.

Towering between the houses in the Ruga Vecchia San Giovanni is the campanile of the church of **San Giovanni Elemosinario** ⑥⑧ (closed), founded in the second half of the 9th century. It too had to be rebuilt after the 1513 fire, and it contains works by Titian's rival Pordenone, by Titian himself and by Domenico Tintoretto.

The Ruga Vecchia San Giovanni and its continuation, the Rughetta del Ravano, are the main

Star Attraction
● the Erberia

> **Hunchback**
> The steps in Campo di Rialto are supported by the crouching figure of the Gobbo di Rialto, the Hunchback of Rialto (by Pietro da Salò, 16th-century). Since the laws of the Republic were proclaimed from the rostrum above, he was identified by Venetians as a citizen weighed down by the burden of state taxes. He represented a safe haven for minor criminals, who were forced to run naked through a hail of blows from San Marco to the Rialto, where they would collapse exhausted at the feet of the little statue.

Looking out from the markets

Map on page 60

Below: Rialto market stalls
Bottom: San Polo

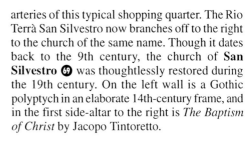

arteries of this typical shopping quarter. The Rio Terrà San Silvestro now branches off to the right to the church of the same name. Though it dates back to the 9th century, the church of **San Silvestro** ⓺ was thoughtlessly restored during the 19th century. On the left wall is a Gothic polyptych in an elaborate 14th-century frame, and in the first side-altar to the right is *The Baptism of Christ* by Jacopo Tintoretto.

CAMPO SAN POLO

The shopping street now comes out into the small Campo Sant' Aponal, with its 11th-century deconsecrated church of **Sant' Apollinare (Aponal)** ⓻ (closed), which was given Gothic additions in the 15th century. At the centre of the church's brick facade, the soaring Gothic style is well displayed by the early 14th-century *Crucifixion* below the window and the late 14th-century relief of the crucifix above it.

Opposite the church, the Calle di Mezzo and the Calle Meloni lead to the bridge across the Rio della Madonetta. The ensuing arcade opens out into the ★★ **Campo San Polo**, one of the largest and most attractive squares in the city.

The church of ★ **San Polo** ⓻ is entered through the Gothic portal in the right transept. The interior of this 9th-century church was restored in the 19th century, and it has a 'ship's keel' roof. On the left of the west door is a fine ★ *Last Supper* by Tintoretto (although the one he did for San Marcuola is better). Tiepolo also provided San Polo with some fine work: his famous ★ *Via Crucis* (Stations of the Cross) can be admired in the Oratory of the Crucifix. In the presbytery there are five large works by Palma il Giovane, which rather upstage the fine 14th-century crucifix with its yellow and gold tones.

Back in the square it's worth taking a look at the **campanile** (1362), with its two fine Romanesque lions; it served as a landmark in the old medieval city for those who had lost their way.

Between the Gothic and the baroque palazzi opposite the church, the Sotoportego dei Cavalli leads out of the campo. One bridge and two corners further ahead, the Calle de la Furatola leads over the bridge of the same name, where there is a fine panorama, before entering the arcade. The first turn-off, the Calle Stretta (Narrow Street), is easy to miss – it comes out in the Campiello Albrizzi with the **palazzo** of the same name, a typical 17th-century Venetian patrician's house that has had its interior preserved as a museum, exhibiting much fine furniture, stucco and paintings (open only for temporary exhibitions).

SAN CASSIANO

Northwest of the Campiello Albrizzi, beyond the Campiello Carampane, the broad shopping street Calle dei Botteri extends as far as the Canal Grande. Halfway there, a street branches off to the left to the church of **San Cassiano 72**.

The interior decoration of this building is not exactly modest; indeed, the altar paintings by Tintoretto are almost swamped by it. His eerie *Crucifixion* on the left wall is almost reminiscent of 19th-century realism. On the right wall is a *Descent into Limbo*. The last altar in the right side-aisle also contains a fine late medieval work which is unfortunately rather badly lit: *St John the Baptist Between Saints*.

Crossing the Rio di San Cassiano now, taking

Star Attraction
● Campo San Polo

Square dances
Campo San Polo was once the site of masked balls, fairs, parades and even bullfights. Today it is the scene of less exotic activities such as cycling and football.

Below: waterbombs in Campo San Polo
Bottom: Campo Santa Maria

Map on page 60

Mystery name
There is no such word as *orio* in Italian, or even in the curious Venetian dialect, so the true meaning of San Giacomo dell' Orio is unclear. The church could have been named after a laurel tree *(alloro)* that grew nearby, though some have suggested that the name could somehow be derived from *lupo* (wolf), as at one time wolves roamed this area.

*Below: palazzo sign
bottom: San Stae facade*

a left turn followed by a right turn, and then crossing a further bridge, we reach the Campo Santa Maria Mater Domini; in the background is the church of the same name, **Santa Maria Mater Domini** ⓗ. The sheer, almost Roman grace and purity of the facade of this High Renaissance building is particularly striking for Venice. The church was consecrated in 1540, and its left transept contains an important *Invention of the Cross* by Tintoretto as well as a fine 13th-century Byzantine bas-relief of the *Madonna in Prayer*.

ORIENTAL ART

The street continues past the church and reaches the rear of the ★★ **Ca' Pésaro** ⓗ *(see page 41)*. This imposing palazzo was built by Baldassare Longhena, Venice's leading 17th-century architect; he modelled it on the Old Library building on the Piazzetta. Yellow signs point the way to the **Galleria d'Arte Moderna** and to the ★ **Museo di Arte Orientale**. Since 1902 the Ca' Pésaro has housed a collection of modern art, and contains works by Utrillo, Rodin, Chagall, Vlaminck, Dufy, Rouault, Matisse, Max Ernst, Klee and Kandinsky. Sadly, the gallery has been closed for restoration since 1983. The Museo di Arte Orientale (open: Tues–Sun 9am–2pm) contains superb collections of Far Eastern art and culture, including fabrics, clothing, armour and porcelain.

SAN GIACOMO

Directly at the entrance to the museum, the narrow Calle di Ca' Pésaro crosses the canal and runs across the Rio di San Stae to the Campo and the church of **San Stae** ⓗ, with its splendid facade facing the Canal Grande. It was built in 1709, and the architecture is neoclassical rather than baroque. The ★ **interior** with its single aisle contains a superb collection of early 18th-century Venetian paintings – a treasure-trove for art-lovers.

The Salizzada di San Stae continues into the Salizzada Carminati, from which the Ramo Carminati branches off to the right and leads across a bridge into the Calle del Colombo. At the end of this street on the left is the down-to-earth ★ **Campo San Giacomo dell'Orio** with its almost refreshing lack of ostentatious facades. The square is dominated by ★★ **San Giacomo dell' Orio** ⓱, a complex consisting of a church and houses dating back to the 9th century. It has been much altered over the centuries, but still has a strong archaic feel to it. To reach the main entrance one has to walk around the huge campanile (13th-century brick).

The church's interior is rather confusing, as the right transept is wider than the left one. If you stand beneath the crossing and follow the course of the 14th-century ★ **ship's keel roof**, the cruciform ground-plan becomes more obvious. In the south transept there is a fine Byzantine column of *verde antico*, and in the crossing is a free-standing ★ **pulpit** in the form of a chalice – its elegant marble intarsias are a Renaissance rarity. The church was altered in the 16th century, and the impessive 14th-century crucifix in the sanctuary was brought here only in 1960.

The Old Sacristy, with its finely carved wood panelling, is entirely decorated with paintings by Palma Giovane (1575). On the left of the exit in the right transept is the entrance to the ★ **Sacrestia Nuova** (New Sacristy). The ceiling paintings are by Paolo Veronese (after 1570).

Star Attractions
● Ca' Pésaro
● San Giacomo dell'Orio

Below: ship's keel roof, San Giacomo dell'Orio
Bottom: Campo San Giacomo

Maps
on page
60 & below

*Waiting at the Scuola Grande
di San Giovanni*

SCUOLA GRANDE DI SAN GIOVANNI

In the middle of the row of facades facing the church, the Calle del Tintor leaves the Campo. Shortly before the bridge (Ponte del Parrucchetta) it is worth taking a small detour off to the left for a glimpse of the **Campo San Boldo**: here a ruined campanile has been integrated into a residential block, and the scene is idyllic.

After the bridge the Rio Terrà Primo leads to the Rio Terrà Secondo, which turns to the right across a bridge into the Calle di Ca' Donà; this comes out in the Campo San Stin.

Cross this square diagonally to reach the ★ **Scuola Grande di San Giovanni Evangelista** ⓲. This *scuola (see page 10)* dates back to 1216. The first court has a beautiful marble screen and portal by Pietro Lombardo (1481). The facade on the left-hand side of the second court is 14th-century Gothic, while the entrance to the *scuola*, with its double windows, is Renaissance (open: Sun and Mon 10am–4pm).

THE FRARI

The Calle del Caffettier and the Calle del Magazzen lead to the Rio Terrà S Tomà behind the Archivio di Stato. Two bridges lead to the Campo dei Frari and to the church of ★★★ **Santa Maria Gloriosa dei Frari** ⓲ (open: Mon–Sat 9am–6pm, Sun 1–6pm). Usually known simply as 'the Frari', this is one of the few Gothic churches in Venice. Despite its simple Franciscan style, the church was a popular burial-place for families, and as a result received a whole series of works of art. It is the home of three of Italy's greatest Renaissance masterpieces.

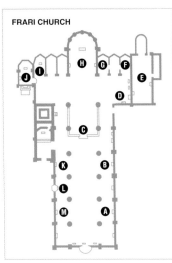

FRARI CHURCH

A Tomb for Titian (c 1488–1576), erected in 1852.

B Sculpture of Bible translator Hieronymus, by Alessandro Vittoria (1560) in the style of Titian.

C ★ **Marble choir screens** (1468–75)

by Bartolomeo Bon, originally Late Gothic and completed in the Early Renaissance style by Pietro Lombardo; ★ **choir stalls** with elaborate carving by Marco Cozzi from Vicenza (1468).

D Monument to General Jacopo Marcello, with the yellow-red-brown flag of St Mark; in front of the entrance to the sacristy, the fine Late Gothic tomb of Pacifico Bon (1437) who probably built the church.

E Sacristy. To the right of the entrance, a marble tabernacle attributed to Pietro Lombardo (1479); opposite, an elaborate baroque altar for reliquaries (1711); the triptych in the Cappella Pesaro (Pesaro chapel) is a masterpiece by Giovanni Bellini: ★★★ *Madonna and Child Between Saints* (1488).

F ★ **Polyptych** (1482) by Bartolomeo Vivarini, in its original frame.

G Cappella dei Fiorentini containing a masterpiece by Donatello in the altar niche, his wooden statue of ★ *St John the Baptist* (1451).

H Sanctuary, with Titian's ★★★ *Assumption*, an incomparable work painted between 1516 and 1518, his first important religious commission.

I Cappella dei Milanesi, containing the tomb of the composer and former music director of St Mark's, Claudio Monteverdi (1643).

J ★ **Cappella Corner**; Late Gothic addition by

Star Attractions
- Santa Maria Gloriosa dei Frari
- Bellini's Madonna and Child
- Titian's Assumption

Simple style
The Franciscan mendicant order arrived in Venice in 1222, received building land in 1250 and spent more than a century from 1340 onwards constructing Santa Maria Gloriosa dei Frari. The choir was not consecrated until 1469. Both the facade and the architecture of the interior reflect the Franciscan order's taste for simplicity, functionality and the absence of superfluous decoration: brick is the dominant material, rather than marble or gold.

Canova's tomb, the Frari

Maps on pages 60, 66 & 69

the Corner family (from 1417). Monument to Federico Corner (Tuscan); stoup with statue of *St John the Baptist* by Sansovino (1554); on the altar, *St Mark Enthroned* by Bartolomeo Vivarini (1474); 15th-century stained-glass windows.

K ★★★ *Madonna di Ca' Pesaro* by Titian (1526), showing the Madonna and Child with saints before members of the Pesaro family.

L Tomb of Doge Giovanni Pesaro by Baldassare Longhena (1669), a bizarre and rather over-laden baroque work.

M Tomb of Canova (1827), designed by the sculptor himself (as a mausoleum for Titian) and carved after his death in 1822.

The church is only part of the complex: the Archivio di Stato (State Archives, containing the documents of the Republic until its end in 1797) are housed in the two cloisters adjoining it. The mighty **campanile** (the second highest in the city after San Marco) was completed in 1396.

SAN ROCCO

The Campo San Rocco contains a fine group of Renaissance buildings, including the church of **San Rocco** ⓐ, which, though begun in 1489, had its lines adapted to suit the Scuola Grande

Below: the Frari campanile
Bottom: San Rocco facade

di San Rocco in the neoclassical style of the late 18th century (1765–71). The church contains some valuable works by Tintoretto in its sanctuary and organ loft.

The facade of the ★★ **Scuola Grande di San Rocco** ③ (open Dec–Feb: Mon–Fri 10am–1pm, Sat and Sun 10am–4pm; Mar and Nov: daily 10am–4pm; Apr–Oct: daily 9am–5pm) is the work of two famous architects: Bartolomeo Bon (died 1529) from Bergamo designed the building and completed the ground floor with its playful, arched windows; Scarpagnino (died 1549) continued working on the building in 1535 and was responsible for adding the extravagant main facade.

The interior is world-famous for its paintings by Jacopo Tintoretto. On the ground floor, the traditional reception room of the *scuole*, Tintoretto painted scenes from the New Testament: (from the left) *Annunciation, Adoration of the Magi, Flight into Egypt, Slaughter of the Innocents, Mary Magdalene, St Mary of Egypt, Circumcision* and the *Assumption*. The rather gloomy room inspired Tintoretto's clever use of light and colour.

The grand staircase by Scarpagnino (1544–46) has two huge paintings commemorating the end of the plague epidemics of 1576 and 1630, and it leads into the huge ★★ **Chapter House**.

This vast room, with its many paintings, conveys a marvellous sense of unity and harmony; the floor and the altar with Tintoretto's *Glorification of St Roch* (1588) contrast with the rhythm of the ceiling frescoes on Old Testament themes. The wall frescoes are devoted to the New Testament.

Star Attractions
● Titian's Madonna di Ca' Pesaro
● Scuola Grande di San Rocco

Venetian master
Jacopo Tintoretto (1518–94) was a true Venetian: apart from a brief stay with his brother in Mantua when he was an old man, he never left the city. His art can be found all over Venice, but his pre-eminent work remains the cycle of more than 50 paintings in the Scuola Grande di San Rocco. Tintoretto (his name means 'little dyer' or 'colourist') enjoyed the patronage of this *scuola* for 23 years.

The Assumption of the Virgin

Ceiling paintings
1 *Moses Striking Water from the Rock*
2 *The Fall of Man*
3 *God the Father Appearing to Moses*
4 *Crossing the Red Sea*
5 *The Rescue of Jonah*
6 *The Miracle of the Bronze Serpent*
7 *The Vision of Ezekiel*
8 *Jacob's Ladder*
9 *The Sacrifice of Isaac*

SCUOLA S. ROCCO (MAIN HALL)

10   *Manna Falling from Heaven*
11   *Elijah in the Wilderness*
12   *Elijah's Miracle of the Loaves*
13   *The Feast of the Passover*

Wall paintings
I   *St Roch*
II   *St Sebastian*
III   *Nativity*
IV   *Baptism of Christ*
V   *Resurrection*
VI   *Agony in the Garden*
VII   *Last Supper*
VIII *Miracle of the Loaves and Fishes*
IX   *Lazarus Raised From the Dead*
X   *Ascension*
XI   *Miracle of Christ at the Pool of Bethesda*
XII   *Temptation of Christ* (with Tintoretto's self-portrait beneath it, 1573).

*Below: The Glory of St Roch
Bottom: The Crucifixion*

In the adjoining Sala d'Albergo, Tintoretto devoted his wall paintings to the Passion; on the ceiling can be seen his *The Glory of St Roch* (or Rocco, the French-born patron saint of the *scuola*) and on the far wall ★★★ *The Crucifixion,* the most moving work of the whole cycle and one of the masterpieces of Italy. Tintoretto worked from 1564 until 1588 on these paintings, which are to Venice what the Sistine Chapel is to Rome.

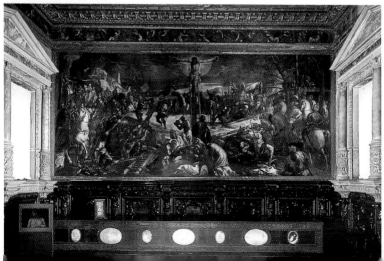

CASA DI GOLDONI

Near the campanile of the Frari Church is a small street, the Calle Larga Prima, that leads behind the **Scuola dei Calegheri (Calzolai)** ③ to the Campo San Tomà. The facade of this 15th-century Cobblers' Guild contrasts with the opulence of San Rocco. The neoclassical church of **San Tomà** ② (1742) completes the scene.

A few steps away, left of the church and over the bridge of San Tomà, is the **Casa di Goldoni** ③. This Gothic building was the birthplace of Venice's great writer of comedies, Carlo Goldoni (born 1707). The house is part-museum, part-institute (and closed for renovation).

The route now runs parallel to the facade of San Tomà and off to the right to the Rio della Frescada. Before you reach the bridge, turn right and cross the rio at the next bridge, which leads via a narrow lane to the Calle Larga Foscari. After the bridge over the Rio Foscari the interior courtyard of the **Ca' Foscari** ④, the University of Venice *(see page 44)*, comes into view.

CA' REZZONICO

The street opens out into a picturesque little square, and the Calle dell Cappeller leads off it. After a right and then a left the street emerges at the Rio di San Barnaba and follows the left bank as far as the ★★ **Ca' Rezzonico** ③. This baroque building by Baldassare Longhena is home to the **Museo del Settecento Veneziano** (Museum of 18th-century Venice), which contains a variety of elegant artefacts: stucco, marble, tapestries, ceramics, fine furniture, and valuable frescoes, including those by Tiepolo, father and son. On the third floor is a reconstruction of an 18th-century apothecary's shop and a puppet theatre.

The bridge over the Rio di San Barnaba is followed by the campo and the church of **San Barnaba** ③, a neoclassical edifice dating from 1749, with a fine 14th-century ★ **campanile**. Calle del Traghetto to the right of the church leads to the Ca' Rezzonico landing-stage, connecting with San Marco and the Rialto.

Star Attractions
● Tintoretto's paintings
● Ca' Rezzonico

Death in Venice
The Ca' Rezzonico was once owned by Robert Browning's reprobate son, Pen, and his wealthy American heiress wife. It was while the poet was staying with them in 1889 that he died of bronchitis in the small apartment on the first floor.

A Madonna outside Casa Goldoni

Map
on page
73

5: Artistic Glories

San Zaccaria – San Giorgio Maggiore – Giudecca – Redentore – Zattere – Punta della Dogana – Santa Maria della Salute – Collezione Guggenheim – Accademia – Santo Stefano

This route visits the islands of the Giudecca and San Giorgio Maggiore, each with a lovely Palladian church, and the superb art collections of the Accademia and the Guggenheim.

Travel by *vaporetto* (water-bus) line 82 from San Zaccaria, west of San Marco, to the Isola di San Giorgio Maggiore. You disembark in front of the church of ★★ **San Giorgio Maggiore ⑧⑦** (open: daily 9.30am–12.30pm and 2.30–6pm). Benedictine monks have lived here since 982, though the present-day complex is mostly Renaissance and inextricably linked with the architect Andrea Palladio. Baldassare Longhena added the double staircase and the library wing (closed to visitors).

CLASSICAL CHURCH

For the church facade, Palladio resolved the problem posed by the high nave and lower aisles here by intersecting classical temple fronts – one joining the side aisles and the other, grander front superimposed upon it and covering the higher elevation of the nave. Construction work

Reclusive order

The Benedictines of San Giorgio had their land and property (including artworks) confiscated by Napoleon, but a few monks still live in the monastery, maintaining the church and leading a life of seclusion. They made a rare public appearance in 1981 when US President Jimmy Carter was invited to breakfast on San Giorgio while attending a trade summit.

San Giorgio Maggiore rooftops

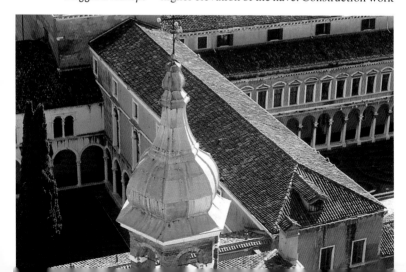

began in 1566 and ended in 1610. The three-aisled ★**interior** is the most spacious and light-filled in the city, and its harmonious proportions make one forget the sheer size of the building. Magnificent artworks here include: first altar on the right, *Adoration of the Shepherds* by Bassano (1592); second altar, *Crucifix* (15th-century); third altar, *Martyrdom of Saints Cosma and Damian* (Tintoretto school); right transept, *Coronation of the Virgin* (Tintoretto school); main altar, bronze group of the *Saviour on a Globe Borne by the Evangelists* (Campagna, 1591–93); right-hand wall, ★*Last Supper*, masterpiece by Tintoretto; left wall, *Manna from Heaven* by Tintoretto. Chapel to the left of the main altar, *Resurrection* (Tintoretto school); left transept, *St Stephen Martyr* (Tintoretto school).

Star Attractions
● San Giorgio church
● Redentore

From the campanile (1791) there is a superb view of the city (lift to the top). In the monastery garden is the Teatro Verde open-air theatre, which reopened in 1999 for the Biennale.

The monastery has preserved an age-old cultural tradition as the seat of the *Fondazione Cini*, an artistic and scientific study centre founded in 1951 by the arts patron Count Vittorio Cini.

THE GIUDECCA

Before reboarding the water-bus it is worth stopping to appreciate the panorama of San Marco across the water. At the next landing-stage, Zitelle, there is another building by Palladio, the church of **Le Zitelle** ❽, a former hostel for girls, and today an exhibition and congress centre. This facade of Palladio's has been much imitated.

The walk along **La Giudecca** here affords superb views of the opposite side of the canal. House No 43 is the **Casa dei Tre Oci (Occhi)** ❽ (Three Eyes), an Art Nouveau structure influenced by Venetian Gothic, which takes its name from three round windows.

After the bridge comes the square in front of the ★★**Redentore** ❾, one of Venice's two plague churches (open: Mon–Sat 10am–5pm, Sun 1–5pm). During the epidemic of 1576, in which

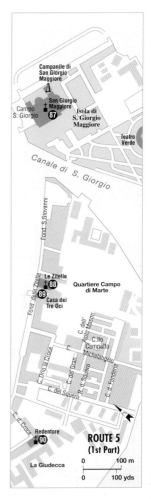

Maps
on pages
73 & 75

Holy dolls
In a small chapel on the left-hand side of Santa Maria del Rosario (I Gesuati) are large dolls of the Madonna and Child, which on feast days are dressed in dazzling jewels and elaborate costumes — including, it is said, lace underwear for the *bambino*.

Below: Il Redentore dome
Bottom: finding the way

Titian died, this building was commissioned by the Republic as a vow to God the Redeemer *(Redentore)*. For the facade Palladio employed the same ingenious solution he used for San Giorgio Maggiore. The interior is not as bright, but the ★ apse is a stroke of genius, lit from the dome above and from the choir, which stands behind a semicircle of Corinthian columns. In the sacristy (entered via the choir) there is a fine *Madonna* by Alvise Vivarini (late 15th-century).

On the third Saturday in July, the feast of the Redentore, a bridge of boats is constructed and a firework display is held in honour of the church's foundation.

I GESUATI

Reboard the water-bus which stops at Palanca before crossing over the Zattere. The facade of the church of ★ **Santa Maria del Rosario** or **I Gesuati** ❿ (open: daily 8am–noon and 5–7pm), despite its conventional neoclassicism, dominates all the others. The ★★ **interior** contains several magnificent 18th-century paintings. The statues between the side-altars go right round the room, and the bas-reliefs above them point the way towards the wonderful ceiling: Tiepolo's superb **fresco** (1737–39) is surrounded by monochrome contributions from his school. The ingenious use of colour, perspective and light here is typical of Tiepolo. The paintings in the side-altars maintain this high standard: in the first altar on the right, *Virgin with Three Saints* by Tiepolo (1740); second altar, *St Dominic* by Piazzetta (1743); third altar, *St Vincent Ferrer, Hyacinth and Ludovico Bertrando* by Piazzetta (1739); first altar on the left, *Pius V and Saints* by Ricci (1732–34); second altar, *The Virgin Mary* (neoclassical, 19th-century); third altar, *Crucifixion* by Tintoretto (1555–60). The elaborate high altar (18th-century) is encased in lapis lazuli.

A few metres to the left of I Gesuati is the less pompous facade of the tiny church of **Santa Maria della Visitazione o San Gerolamo dei Gesuati**, with its fine Lombardesque decoration (1494–1524).

WATERSIDE WALK

On the Campo Sant'Agnese is the church of **Sant' Agnese ❷** (open Sun am only). Its exterior is Veneto-Byzantine (12th to 13th-century), with simple lines, rounded arches and brickwork. The fresco fragments inside once formed part of its decoration (13–14th-century).

One of the nicest walks in Venice is along the **Zattere** – a perfect location for a leisurely drink or ice-cream. From a distance the facades of San Giorgio Maggiore and the Redentore on the Giudecca opposite look as if they are part of a painting. The **Magazzini del Sale ❸** were the Republic's old salt warehouses; today they are open to visitors only when exhibitions are held.

Every ship that used the Canal Grande in the old days had to pass the **Punta della Dogana ❹**. At the extreme end of the promontory the little turret surmounted by a golden ball with a weathervane

Star Attraction
● I Gesuati interior

Ice-cream along the Zattere

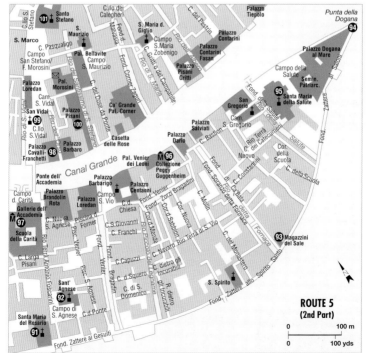

Map on page 75

of Fortune supported by two telamones (designed by Falcone, late 17th-century) became a landmark. The view from here is always breathtaking.

SANTA MARIA DELLA SALUTE

The route continues along the city's old customs houses, and soon the church of ★★ **Santa Maria della Salute** ⓖ, Venice's second plague church, comes into view (open: daily 9am–noon and 3–6pm). Consecrated in 1687, it is one of Venice's most distinctive landmarks and a superb example of Venetian baroque architecture. It was commissioned by the Republic as a vow to God during the epidemic of 1630, and of the 11 designs submitted, the one by Baldassare Longhena was chosen. The octagonal building, more a votive temple than a church, has a huge dome, and sculptured figures standing on volutes act as buttresses. The high dome with its drum and large windows sheds a beautiful light on the interior with its circular aisle.

Below: the Fortune weather vane
Bottom: the Salute from the Lagoon

The three altars to the right of the entrance are masterpieces by Luca Giordano (late 17th-century); third altar to the left, *Descent of the Holy Spirit* by Titian (1555). Presbytery: colossal marble altar, *Virgin Casting out the Plague*, designed by Longhena. Sacristy: over the altar, *St Mark Enthroned Between Saints Cosma and Damian, and Saints Roch and Sebastian* (1512); on the side

walls, eight roundels (the Four Evangelists and Doctors of the Church) by Titian. Altar frontal: valuable 15th-century tapestry. The wall opposite the entrance, *Marriage at Cana* by Tintoretto (1551). Beneath it, *St Sebastian* by Basaiti (early 16th-century), a fine Early Renaissance work. On the ceiling, *Cain and Abel, Sacrifice of Isaac,* and *David and Goliath,* all by Titian.

Before the bridge over Rio della Salute there is a view of the apse of the former ★ **Abbazia di San Gregorio** (closed to the public). This Gothic building was designed by Antonio Cremonese (mid-15th century); bricks were used for its simple exterior decoration. The door and windows are unaltered.

GUGGENHEIM COLLECTION

The Calle Bastion crosses the Rio delle Fornaci and bends left into a campiello, from which a bridge leads to the Palazzo Venier dei Leoni, home of the ★★ **Collezione Peggy Guggenheim** ⑨⑥ (open: Wed–Mon 10am–6pm, Sat in summer 10am–10pm). This is Venice's leading contemporary art museum, with a superb collection of works by Picasso, Braque, Chagall, Kandinsky, Bacon, Pollock and many more. The late Peggy Guggenheim (1898–1979) had a particular interest in Surrealism, especially as she was briefly married to one of the movement's founders, Max Ernst. He is well represented here, along with Dali, Magritte and de Kooning.

THE ACCADEMIA

The Fondamenta Venier leads away from the gallery and along a pretty canal until it comes out in the Campo San Vio. Across the Rio San Vio and along the Piscina Forner is the ★★★ **Gallerie dell'Accademia** ⑨⑦ (entrance on the canal front; open: Tues–Sun 8.15am–7.15pm, Mon 9am–2pm). The 24 rooms contain the most complete and important collection of Venetian painting from the 14th–18th century, a collection that Napoleon moved here to the former convent of Santa Maria della Carità in 1807, and augmented

Star Attractions
● Santa Maria della Salute
● Collezione Peggy Guggenheim
● Gallerie dell'Accademia

Eccentric palace
The Palazzo Venier, once the home of the American Peggy Guggenheim and now of the modern art collection that bears her name, was built in the 18th century for the noble Venier family, and soon nicknamed the *nonfinito*, because it was never completed beyond the first floor. It is a splendidly eccentric setting for the collection, with a lovely garden and courtyard that was once the home of chained lions – hence the palazzo's soubriquet 'dei Leoni'. Peggy Guggenheim preferred dogs to lions, and many of them are buried in the sculpture garden alongside her own grave.

A Guggenheim exhibit

Map on page 75

Early start
The Accademia is illuminated by natural light, so choose a bright day to see the works at their best. And try to be at the gallery around opening time. The later you leave it, the more crowded it will be, especially in high season, when there are sometimes long queues to see some of the paintings.

Tintoretto's 'Miracle of St Mark' in the Accademia

by treasures removed from Venice's convents, monasteries and churches. The rooms are arranged chronologically, beginning with Byzantine and Gothic influences. Highlights include Paolo Veneziano's stunning *Coronation of the Virgin* (1325). The 15th century is represented by works of Carpaccio and Giovanni Bellini, while the 16th century displays the golden age of Venetian painting, symbolised by the trio of Veronese, Tintoretto and Titian. The 17th and 18th centuries' masters are crowned perhaps by Tiepolo, the greatest 18th-century Venetian artist.

Palazzo Pisani

From the wooden Ponte dell'Accademia there are fine views of the Canal Grande and the Late Gothic facade of the **Palazzo Cavalli-Franchetti** ⑱, with its geometrically arranged arches. On the opposite bank is the deconsecrated church of **San Vitale** ⑲, which dates from the 11th century. The facade was built in the Palladian style by Andrea Tirali in around 1700. There are valuable paintings inside, including Carpaccio's *San Vitale*.

The enormous **Palazzo Pisani** ⑩, which today houses the Conservatory of Music, is one of the largest private palaces in Venice. Begun in 1614, it has two interior courtyards divided by a huge open-arched loggia (closed to the public).

Santo Stefano

The Campo Francesco Morosini (commonly called the Campo Santo Stefano) was the scene of the city's last ever *Caccia al toro* (bullfight) in 1802. In this popular square is the church of ★ **Santo Stefano** ⑩ (open: Mon–Sat 10am– 5pm, Sun 1–5pm), with its magnificent Gothic portal by the Bartolomeo Bon workshop. The church dates back to the 13th century, but was later rebuilt in Gothic style. The sacristy contains three fine works by Tintoretto: *The Last Supper*, *Washing of the Feet* and *Prayer in the Garden* (16th-century). The leaning campanile, built in 1544, is a familiar part of the city skyline.

6: Cannaregio

Ferrovia – San Giobbe – Ghetto Nuovo – Madonna dell'Orto – Abbazia della Misericordia – San Marziale – Ca' d'Oro

Map
on page
80

The most northerly of the six *sestieri*, Cannaregio is also the least explored. Its lovely wide canals and quiet backstreets seem far from the hubbub of St Mark's and the Rialto.

Towering next to Santa Lucia railway station is the facade of the **Santa Maria degli Scalzi** ⑩, a neoclassical building designed by Giuseppe Sardi and consecrated in 1705. The interior is by Baldassare Longhena. During World War I this church lost its painted ceiling by Tiepolo (the two surviving fragments can be seen in the Accademia, *see page 78*). The interior is profusely decorated; the second chapel on the right and the third on the left contain frescoes by Tiepolo.

Below: Santa Maria degli Scalzi
Bottom: a Cannaregio canal

PALAZZO LABIA

The Lista di Spagna, the busy street in front of the station, leads to the Campo San Geremia with the church of the same name and also the pompous **Palazzo Labia** ⑩. The Labia family spent a fortune on their palazzo, and around the middle of the 18th century they employed some of the most famous painters around: Tiepolo, who was at the

Map
below

height of his powers, produced some superb frescoes. The ★**Salone** (ballroom) contains his frescoes of *Antony and Cleopatra*; the decoration of the entire room is magnificently harmonious. (Visits by prior arrangement, tel: 041 524 2812.)

San Giobbe

SAN GIOBBE

The path on the left-hand side of the Canale di Cannaregio leads to **San Giobbe 104**, an Early Renaissance church started by Antonio Gambello in 1450 and enlarged by Pietro Lombardo.

The fine marble intarsia on the portal is continued in the interior. The area around the domed sanctuary is particularly elaborate; the *Evangelists* in the pendentives are the work of Lombardo himself. In the second altars on the right and left respectively there is some fine marble, and the vault of the left one is also lined with majolica tiles and roundels: *Christ and the Evangelists*.

The Cappella Contarini (after the fourth altar on the right) shows traces of the previous Gothic building by Antonio Gambello (mid-15th century); on the altar, *Presepio* (Nativity) by Gerolamo Savoldo (1540). The sacristy contains an *Annunciation* triptych by Antonio Vivarini (*circa* 1445).

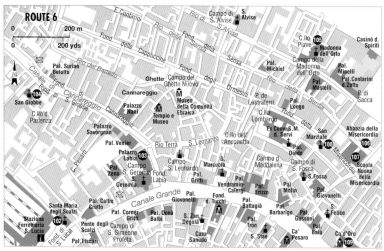

THE GHETTO

Cross the 17th-century ★ **Ponte dei Tre Archi** ('Three-Arched Bridge'), turn right and walk down the side of the Canale di Cannaregio until signs appear pointing the way to the **Ghetto**. In 1527 the Republic gave the Jews – who were tolerated and an important part of the city's economic life – permission to inhabit the part of the city formerly occupied by the iron foundry *(getto)*. They built synagogues, schools and seven-storey tenement blocks, building upwards to overcome the lack of space in this enclosed area, which became known as Ghetto Nuovo. The 'new ghetto' is in fact the world's oldest.

MADONNA DELL'ORTO

A wrought-iron bridge leads from the Ghetto Nuovo to the Fondamenta Ormesini. The straight canals here with their continuous quays and views out to the lagoon are typical of the Cannaregio quarter of the city. The Calle della Malvasia connects with the next canal, the Rio della Sensa; next on the right comes the Campo dei Mori. The Venetians' general term for anything foreign to them was *moro* (Moorish), and on the house on the corner to the right there are three *Mori* statues set into the outside wall.

The campo and church of ★★ **Madonna dell' Orto** ⓪⑤ (open: Mon–Sat 10am–5pm, Sun 1–5pm) are named after a miraculous statue of the Madonna which was found in a nearby orchard *(orto)*. Jacopo Tintoretto (1518–94), one of the greatest painters of all time, lies buried here. The brick facade is a fine example of Venetian Late Gothic (1462). The round arches at the centre already presage the Renaissance. The statues of the Apostles in the niches are by the Delle Masegne.

In the three-aisled interior there are some superb works by Tintoretto, notably *St Agnes Raising Licinius* (1569) in the fourth chapel of the left side-aisle, and *The Presentation of the Virgin in the Temple* (1552) in the Cappella di San Mauro. A modest slab in the chapel to the right of the choir marks Tintoretto's resting-place.

Star Attraction
● Madonna dell'Orto

Jewish Museum
The **Museo Comunità Ebraica** on the Campo di Ghetto Nuovo contains some valuable cultural artefacts (daily except Sat and Jewish holidays 10am–5.30pm). Synagogue tours in English and Italian also start from here (every hour 10.30am–4.30pm, daily except Fri, Sat and Jewish holidays; hours might vary, tel: 041 715 359).

Below: detail from the Ghetto
Bottom: Tintoretto's house

Map on page 80

Ancient bridge
Going left over the bridge opposite the Scuola Nuova della Misericordia, you will see a tiny bridge with no parapet, leading to a house. This is the oldest bridge in the city (13th-century) and is a typical Venetian construction with segmented arches and shallow steps.

The Misericordia Abbazia, church and bridge

LA MISERICORDIA

The route continues along the canal as far as the Sacca della Misericordia, and then turns right; before the bridge over the Rio della Sensa, the Fondamenta dell'Abbazia leads off to the left towards the campo, and then left again to the **Abbazia della Misericordia** ⓾, built in the 15th century. The Late Gothic facade used to be that of the Scuola Vecchia della Misericordia, one of the city's six major confraternities *(see page 10)*. Unfortunately, the building is in urgent need of repair, as is the adjoining church of the former abbey dating from 1659.

Across the wooden bridge is a huge brick building designed by Jacopo Sansovino in 1534: the **Scuola Nuova della Misericordia** ⓭, the new *scuola*. The exterior was never completed.

VEGETABLE STALLS

On the path that runs beside the Rio della Misericordia stands the Palazzo Lezze, designed by Longhena in 1654. Passing the church of **San Marziale** ⓭, take the third bridge: the Calle dell'Aseo comes out into the Campiello dell' Anconetta with its neo-Gothic Teatro Italia, once a cinema. Over the Rio Terrà Maddalena is the Campo of the same name with the round 18th-century church. Looking right from the portal,

there is a fine view across the rooftops. The shopping street after the bridge is the Strada Nova, where there are stalls selling lots of mouthwatering fruit and vegetables.

Star Attraction
● Ca' d'Oro

CA' D'ORO

The ★★**Ca' d'Oro** ⑩ is the finest Venetian Gothic palace in the city *(see also page 42)*. The lace-like facade, with its ogee windows, carved capitals, crowning pinnacles and bas-reliefs, was once covered in gold leaf – hence the name, House of Gold. Today the palace contains the **Galleria Franchetti**, an important art gallery (open: daily 8.15am–2pm).

Below: a gaggle of tourists and gondolas
Bottom: the Ca' d'Oro courtyard

The interior has suffered many changes over the years and is barely recognisable as a15th-century palace. The courtyard – where the stairway that used to adorn the exterior is preserved – is decorated with numerous works of art including the marble well-head by the man who built the palace, Bartolomeo Bon.

Baron Franchetti, who bequeathed his palace and collection to the state in 1916, had collected valuable paintings, tapestries and sculpture from every epoch. His favourite piece was Mantegna's famous *St Sebastian (circa* 1500), now on the first floor. Fifteenth-century Venetian bronzes and sculptures stand in the portico, which stretches the length of the palace as far as the loggia. Notable works are Tullio Lombardo's sculpted portrait of *The Young Couple* and the *Madonna and Child* marble lunette by Sansovino.

Fragments of frescoes by Titian and Giorgione from the Fondaco dei Tedeschi, and also by Pordenone from the monastery of Santo Stefano, can be admired in the second-floor hall; the sculptures in the glass cases are by Bernini and Piazzetta.

The room to the left of the loggia contains a Bordone, a Van Dyck, a Titian and a Tintoretto. The rooms off to the right contain 16th-century Flemish works. The building also houses several panels by masters of the Tuscan school (15th-century). A real gem is the ★**carved staircase** in the side-rooms off to the left.

Map on page 86

7: East of San Marco

San Marco – Riva degli Schiavoni – Scuola di San Giorgio degli Schiavoni – San Francesco della Vigna – San Martino – Arsenale – Isola di San Pietro – Giardini Pubblici

This route through the Sestiere Castello covers many of Venice's highlights – the extraordinary opulence of San Zaccaria, a famous painting of St George and the Dragon, and the former nucleus of Venice's maritime power, the Arsenale.

The Venetians had particularly close ties with the Dalmatian coast, and tended to call all the people across the Adriatic 'Slavs' – a name reflected in the Riva degli Schiavoni (Quay of the Slavs), which runs east from the Molo. First on this route are the **prigioni** (prisons) ⑩, which were built in 1859 and are an essential part of any tour of the Doge's Palace *(see page 38)*. Before the next bridge stands a building worthy of its fine surroundings, the **Palazzo Dandolo**, a Late Gothic structure (15th-century), which since 1822 has been the famous Grand Hotel Danieli.

Privileged sisters

The Benedictine nuns of the former convent of San Zaccaria were well looked after by successive doges. They are said to have donated part of the convent orchard so that Piazza San Marco could be enlarged, and to show gratitude for this gift the doge visited the convent every Easter. The ceremony included the presentation to the doge of the ducal cap, or *cornu*. In the 18th century, the convent was the scene of plays, masquerades and balls that were frequented by the glitterati of Venetian society.

SAN ZACCARIA

San Zaccaria facade

The second turn-off after the bridge, a low *sottoportego* (passage), leads on to the campo and church of ★★ **San Zaccaria** ⑪, which together with its ex-convent makes up a huge complex. The building dates back to the 9th century; its present appearance is the result of the alterations undertaken in the 15th and early 16th century.

The church also retains the 13th-century campanile from the previous building on the site, the Gothic church dating from 1444–65. It was built by Antonio Gambello; he was also entrusted with the new building, which was continued after his death (1481) by Mauro Codussi. The imposing facade thus reflects the work of two very different architects: the two lowest storeys by Gambello are Late Gothic, while the rest of the facade is Early Renaissance, finished by Codussi around 1504. The large round gables are unusual for Venice.

This mix of styles is continued inside the church

in the ambulatory: round Renaissance arches crown Late Gothic pointed-arch arcades, the vault and the capitals recall Byzantine architecture, and the tomb slabs in the floor are Lombardesque. The sculptor Alessandro Vittoria (1524–1608) lies buried on the left-hand side of the ambulatory. He created the statue of the patron saint for the facade, and his graceful *St John the Baptist* can be admired next to the stoup near the entrance. He also designed the second altar to the right, which contains the relics of St Zacharias.

ARTISTIC HIGHLIGHTS

Like many other churches in Venice, San Zaccaria was packed with paintings during the 17th and 18th centuries. Works worthy of attention here include the *Madonna Enthroned* by Bellini (1505) in the second side-altar on the left; in the altar of the chapel of St Athanasius (access to the right of the choir) there is an early Tintoretto, *The Birth of St John the Baptist*; the fine choir stalls are by Marco Cozzi (1455–64), and the magnificent seats here were formerly reserved for the doge.

The ★ **Chapel of St Tarasias** next door (open: Mon–Sat 10am–noon and 4–6pm, Sun 4–6pm) was the apse of the former church and contains fragments of flooring and frescoes as well as three magnificent Gothic altars by Ludovico da Forli

Star Attraction
● San Zaccaria

Below: Tintoretto's 'Birth of John the Baptist'
Bottom: Bellini's 'Madonna Enthroned'

Map below

(1443–44). The three paintings at the huge central altar are by Stefano Plebanus (1385). A stairway leads to the 9th-century crypt, which has subsided below sea-level, so its floor is under water all year round.

The Santa Maria della Pietà interior

LA PIETA

After the next bridge along the Rivà degli Schiavoni there is an unpretentious-looking little church that possesses one of the most harmonious and successful interiors in the whole city: ★ **Santa Maria della Pietà** ⑫, usually called simply La Pietà. Construction was begun in 1745 and the church's conventional facade was designed by Giorgio Massari. But the elliptical ★ **interior** is highly original, and reminiscent of a baroque church, though the style bypassed Venice completely *(see page 107)*.

The interior decoration reflects the consistency of the architecture; the finely worked gilt grilles are cleverly placed to their fullest advantage on the walls and balconies, and the muted pastels of the paintings on the ceiling and above the altar profit greatly from the gentle light they receive. The finest of the work here is by the two great

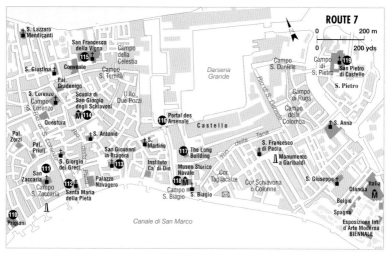

18th-century painters Tiepolo and Piazzetta: Tiepolo painted the ceiling himself, and Piazzetta the high altar, above which there is another work by Tiepolo, the *Four Cardinal Virtues*. The effect of the whole is a masterpiece of architectural and artistic harmony. The church is usually closed in winter, except for evening concerts, although you can sometimes peek in during rehearsals.

SAN GIOVANNI IN BRAGORA

The Calle Pietà runs past the right of the church; it then turns right and after the bridge comes out into the Campo Bandiera e Moro; on one side of this square is the Gothic **Palazzo Gritti-Badoer** (15th-century), and on the other the church of **San Giovanni in Brágora** ⑬ ('in the Marketplace'). Its tripartite brick facade is Gothic in style, presaging the Early Renaissance. The interior contains some wonderful paintings: at the high altar, a *Baptism of Christ* by Cima da Conegliano (1492–94); in the left choir chapel, a triptych of the *Madonna Enthroned* by Bartolomeo Vivarini (1478), and in the first side-chapel to the left, *Christ Resurrected* by Alvise Vivarini.

SCUOLA DI SAN GIORGIO

The Salizzada San Antonin leaves the campo on the right of the palazzo. On the right bank, just past the church of the same name stands the ★★ **Scuola di San Giorgio degli Schiavoni** ⑭ (open: Tues–Sat 9.30am–12.30pm and 3.30–6.30pm, Sun 10am–12.30pm). Today, this two-storey building (its facade was built in 1551) is well-known for its paintings by Vittore Carpaccio (1486–1525).

Above the wooden panelling on the ground floor, scenes from the lives of the three Dalmatian patron saints (George, Tryphon and Jerome) extend all round the room; the paintings were produced between 1507 and 1509. Most famous of them is the ★ *Triumph of St George over the Dragon*. In overcoming the formality and stiffness of medieval painting, Carpaccio's vivacity and realism herald the Early Renaissance.

Star Attraction
● Scuola di San Giorgio

Maestro of Santa Maria
La Pietà is sometimes called 'Vivaldi's church'. It was formerly attached to an orphanage for girls, where the composer was the resident composer, violin teacher and choirmaster between 1704 and 1738. Vivaldi played the organ that still functions in the church and, apart from his operas, most of his compositions from this period were written for La Pietà.

The Scuola di San Giorgio degli Schiavoni

Map on page 86

Mark the spot

San Francesco della Vigna stands on the spot where, according to Venetian legend, an angel appeared to St Mark in a dream, saying *Pax tibi, Marce Evangelista meus* (Peace be with you, Mark, my Evangelist), the motto of the Republic *(see page 21).* A small church consecrated to St Mark stood on this site before the vineyard here was bequeathed to the Franciscan order for a convent.

SAN FRANCESCO DELLA VIGNA

Keep left after the Calle Furlani, then go via the Campo delle Gatte, the Salizzada delle Gatte and the Ramo San Francesco della Vigna to reach the church of **San Francesco della Vigna ⑮**. It was rebuilt by Sansovino in 1534; the facade is by Palladio. The large interior contains the magnificent ★ **Cappella Giustiniani**, left of the high altar, decorated with precious marble from the Pietro Lombardo school (late 15th-century). Surprisingly, the picture of the founder (at the altar) shows an entirely different facade from the actual one by Palladio, in the Lombardesque style.

The left transept provides access to the Cappella Santa, which contains Giovanni Bellini's *Madonna and Four Saints* (1507). There is also a charming *Madonna and Child Enthroned* by Antonio da Negroponte (c 1450) in the right transept. Bring plenty of 200 lire coins to light up the paintings.

San Francesca della Vigna

SAN MARTINO

Take the Calle del Cimitero to the Campo della Celestia, cross the canal to the Campiello Santa Trinità, then cross another canal and turn right into the Calle Magno, which leads to the Campo do Pozzi. Leave this square on the left-hand side for the Rio delle Gorne, which runs along the wall of the Arsenale. On the bank of the canal is the church of **San Martino** which was given its present look by Sansovino in 1540. The unusual feature of its ★ **facade** is that Renaissance architectural forms have been achieved via the use of a very Gothic material: brick. There is no marble to be seen anywhere on this remarkable facade.

THE ARSENALE

From San Martino, the main entrance to the ★ **Arsenale ⑯** is just a few steps away. In former times this was one of the most strongly protected sections of the entire city. It was here that the Venetians protected their monopoly on shipbuilding, for their own and others' use, for trade as well as for war. The dockyard, first used in 1104, grew into an installation covering 32 hectares (79 acres) and by the 16th century was the world's greatest naval shipyard, employing 16,000 workmen.

The great ★★**gateway** in the form of a triumphal arch (1460, by Antonio Gambello) is the earliest example of Renaissance architecture in all Venice. The winged lion and the figure of St Justina, two favourite symbols of the Venetians, stand guard over it. *Justice* dates from 1578; the victory over the Turks at the battle of Lepanto in 1571 turned the gateway to the Arsenal into a memorial, and its decoration was extended with every further victory.

The colossal lion sitting upright on the left was once part of a fountain at the Athenian port of Piraeus; it bears a runic inscription carved in 1040 by Scandinavian mercenaries fighting for Byzantium against Greek rebels. Doge Francesco Morosini (1688–94) had it brought from Athens to Venice as booty, together with the other recumbent lion beside it.

The two towers at the entrance to the canal were built in 1574. Cross the Canale dell'Arsenale now and walk along the other bank as far as the Bacino (Basin) di San Marco. Halfway there the Campo della Tana bears off to the left; the **long building** ⑰ used to contain the *corderie* (rope-making section) of the Arsenal and is now used by the **Biennale** as an exhibition centre *(see page 112)*.

Star Attraction
● **Arsenale gateway**

Below: the Hellenistic lion
Bottom: the Arsenale gateway

Map on page 86

NAVAL HISTORY MUSEUM

On the corner of St Mark's Basin lies the ★ **Museo Storico Navale** ⑱, the Naval History Museum (open: Mon–Sat 8.45am–1.30pm), which houses maritime relics of the Venetian Republic and of the Italian Navy, and also a collection of several thousand sea-shells.

Next comes the little naval church of **San Biagio** (rebuilt in the 18th century) on the campo of the same name, and just after the first bridge is the Via Garibaldi – a filled-in canal that is wider than most of the other medieval streets in the city and so looks rather like a pedestrian precinct. It passes through a lively residential area, and there are several fine views to be had down its side-streets.

Below: the naval museum
Bottom: Castello Canal

SAN PIETRO DI CASTELLO

The Via Garibaldi joins another canal with paths alongside it, the Rio di Sant'Ana; the bridge over the Canale di San Pietro affords a fine view of the various dockyard activities that are so characteristic of this quarter of the city.

The island of **San Pietro**, a small village in itself, was the site of the cathedral of Venice from the 11th century until 1807, when the bishop's see was transferred to the Basilica of San Marco. For this reason, the church of **San Pietro di Castello** ⑲ (open: Mon–Sat 10am–5pm, Sun 1–5pm) is far larger than any village church, since it was the seat of the archbishops of Venice until 1807. The facade, with its pillared portico, is very reminiscent of the style of Palladio, and dates from 1596.

The interior, too, is very Palladian, and the church has undeniable similarities with the Redentore *(see page 73)*. However, the interior decoration is much more elaborate. One of the most interesting features is the marble episcopal throne *(cattedra)* between the second and third side-altars on the right. It is said to have been used by St Peter at Antioch, and there are verses from the Koran and various Islamic motifs on the backrest.

GIARDINI PUBBLICI

On the way back, take the Calle Larga, the other bridge over the Canale di San Pietro; it provides a good general view of the church as a whole, including the gently inclining campanile designed by Mauro Codussi between 1482 and 1488.

The route then continues along the delightful little streets of the Campo di Ruga quarter of the city as far as the Rio di Sant'Ana and back to the Via Garibaldi. Turn left at a small park and you find yourself face-to-face with the **statue of Garibaldi** (1885), the hero of Italian unification. He is standing on a rock with a rather sleepy lion of St Mark in the foreground; the work is by the sculptor Augusto Benvenuti (1838–99). The park then leads on to the **Giardini Pubblici** (Public Gardens), which were laid out on the orders of Napoleon. It is a place for recreation and contains the exhibition pavilions used for the Biennale.

At this point it is worth taking a few extra steps to see the church of **Sant' Isepo** (Venetian for *San Giuseppe*). Its Early Renaissance facade (1512), though in need of restoration, is still a fine piece of work. The perspective ceiling inside is attributed to Giovanni Antonio Torrigli. The imposing tombs of Doge Marino Grimani (1595–1605) and his wife were designed for the side walls by Scamozzi (*circa* 1600). There are also two fine bronze reliefs by Girolamo Campagna.

Grand galley
The most spectacular exhibit in the Naval History Museum is undoubtedly the model of the *Bucintoro*, the name given to the ornate gala ship of the doge, with its 200 oarsmen, that was used for the Ascension festival of the marriage of Venice with the sea *(see page 113)*. Admiral Paolucci had this model made in 1824, shortly before the last of these ships, built in 1728, was destroyed.

The Early Renaissance facade of Sant' Isepo

8: Dorsoduro

Piazzale Roma – San Nicolò da Tolentino – Santa Maria Maggiore – San Nicolò dei Mendicoli – San Sebastiano – Campo Santa Margherita – San Trovaso – San Basilio – Sacca Fisola

The Sestiere Dorsoduro is the longest inhabited part of Venice. *Dorsoduro* means 'hard back', because the clay here is slightly firmer than in the rest of the city, which made it the obvious place for 5th-century refugees from the Germanic tribes to build their first settlements. Today much of this area seems comparatively shabby and run-down, but there are many beautiful churches hiding their art behind a veil of elegant dilapidation.

From the uninspiring car park at the Piazzale Roma, cross the Rio Nuovo into the **Giardini Papadópoli** ⓴, a public park on the site of a church and monastery. Cross the park to reach the Campo dei Tolentini, which is named after its

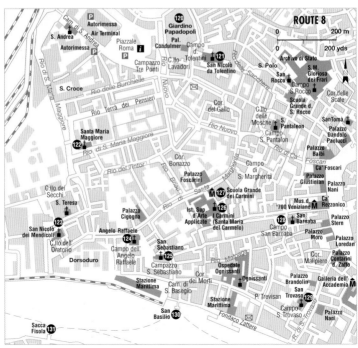

church, **San Nicolò da Tolentino (I Tolentini)** ⓤ. It was built by Scamozzi between 1591 and 1602; its Corinthian portico, based on the Pantheon in Rome, is by Andrea Tirali (1706–14). The interior is conventional neoclassical, and was filled with a wealth of stucco and paintings. On the left wall of the high altar, the tomb of the great Venetian admiral Francesco Morosini (died 1694) is noteworthy for its colossal 'curtain' made of marble, a work by Filippo Parodi, a pupil of Bernini.

On the left side of the bank, walk past the church and up to a bridge; after this, keep to the right and follow the other canal as far as a large wooden bridge, one of several bridges over the various canals that intersect here (this area is known as Tre Ponti). After the wooden bridge go left along the side of the canal, and turn right on the Rio di Santa Maria Maggiore as far as the church of **Santa Maria Maggiore** ⓤ. Today the church and its convent are used as a prison.

I MENDICOLI

Cross the bridge on the long side of the church and then take the first street on the right to reach the Fondamenta del Arzere; from there, the second bridge leads to the Fondamenta Teresa; turn left off it and across to the church of ★★**San Nicolò dei Mendicoli** ⓤ (open: Mon–Sat 9am–5pm, Sun 1–5pm). This church dates from the Early Middle Ages (7th century) and many believe that a pagan temple may once have stood on this site. The present structure, which from the outside resembles a three-aisled basilica, dates back to the 12th century; above the round window in the facade a Byzantine double-window can just be made out. The portico was reconstructed in the 15th century using old material; the 14th-century nave assumed its present appearance only in 1580. The gilded wooden panelling, statues and paintings on the walls and ceilings all combine to form a fine Renaissance interior; from the high altar the pointed arches of the last two arcades can be seen. The apse was part of the original 12th-century building. The 12th-century cam-

Ancient rivalry
San Nicolò dei Mendicoli was once the foremost church on this side of the Grand Canal. Inhabitants of the three western *sestieri* – Dorsoduro, Santa Croce and San Polo – called themselves Nicolotti, and in this church elected their 'Doge dei Nicolotti', who would lead them in their regattas, races, games and often brawls against the eastern half of the population, known as Castellani, after their headquarters in Castello.

Opposite: statue on Giardini Papadópoli
Below: San Nicolò dei Mendicoli

Map
on page
92

Below: Angelo Raffaele
statues
Bottom: Othello's house,
Campo dei Carmini

panile seems particularly massive and cumbersome because it was never given a proper top.

On the other side of it is the Rio di San Nicolò, and the second bridge along it leads across to the church of **Angelo Raffaele** ㉔. The church's organ loft is directly above its canal-side entrance; the parapet is decorated with some superb ★ **paintings** by Antonio Guardi (brother of the more famous Francesco) dating from 1750–53. Here he depicts the story of Tobias and the archangel Raphael.

SPLENDOUR OF VERONESE

Leave the church now via the side entrance, keep to the left and cross the square. ★★ **San Sebastiano** ㉕ (open: Mon–Sat 10am–5pm) is the burial-place of the great painter Paolo Veronese (1530–88). The ceiling here is worthy of the Doge's Palace: elaborately carved, it provides the perfect setting for paintings by Veronese (1556).

He painted the large work above the high altar, *Madonna and Child with St Sebastian*, around 1560; the magnificent organ panels are also by him; the paintings on the walls of the altar date from 1565; Veronese himself lies beneath the organ to the right. The door beneath the organ loft leads to the sacristy, where Veronese demonstrated his genius in 1555 by painting its ceiling: after passing the test here on a small scale he was allowed to do the rest of the church too.

I CARMINI

The church portal faces a bridge; cross it then turn left along the canal bank, which leads to the Campo dei Carmini with the Casa di Otello (Othello's House, closed to the public) at No. 2615.

I Carmini (Santa Maria del Carmelo) ㉖ is the name of the former Carmelite church; its three-aisled basilica is separated by 24 pillars (14th-century). The ornate decoration of the interior, with its gilded wood panelling and paintings, dates mainly from the 17th century. In the second side-altar to the right is a *Presepio* (Nativity) by

Cima da Conegliano (1509), and opposite it is a painting famous for its gentle landscape, *San Nicolò* by Lorenzo Lotto (1529). The ★ **side exit** next to it needs to be appreciated from outside the building: it is characteristically Gothic (14th-century), but contains Byzantine elements (11th to 13th-century).

Star Attractions
● San Sebastiano
● Campo Santa Margherita

AROUND CAMPO SANTA MARGHERITA

Opposite the church is the ★ **Scuola Grande dei Carmini** ㉗, today a gallery (open: Mon–Sat 9am–6pm, Sun 9am–4pm) noted for its cycle of paintings dedicated to the Madonna del Carmine (of the Carmelites). A staircase decorated with magnificent stucco leads into the *Salone*, with its nine fine ceiling paintings by Tiepolo dating from 1739–44, when he was at the height of his powers; light, space and colour all blend together perfectly in these works.

As far as the other paintings here are concerned, special mention must be made of Piazzetta's incredibly expressive *Judith and Holofernes* (in the Room of the Archives, by the door).

Like all the large squares in the city, the ★★ **Campo Santa Margherita** is very distinctive, with medieval buildings, the seemingly sawn-off campanile at the other end, and a small market. No. 2931 is noteworthy for its use of the pointed

Sociable square
Campo Santa Margherita was once the marketplace of Dorsoduro and is still the vibrant social centre of the *sestiere*. The shops here sell food and household goods, rather than souvenirs, and there are numerous local bars and restaurants with tables outside – a good place to enjoy a relatively cheap snack and observe the everyday life of the city.

Tiepolo's ceiling paintings, Scuola Grande dei Carmini

Map
on page
92

Gondola yard
Opposite San Trovaso, at the junction of two canals, is one of Venice's last remaining *squeri* (gondola boatyards). This one dates from the 17th century, and gondolas are still made, repaired and cleaned here, for the city's 400 or so full-time *gondolieri*. There is no shortage of advance orders for these enduring symbols of Venice; each gondola costs around 10,500 euros (£6,500), and the craftsmanship is of the highest quality.

Gondola yard on
Rio San Trovaso

moresco arch. The isolated building in the centre of the square was once the tanners' *scuola*; the worn relief of the *Virgin* with the brothers of the confraternity on the wall dates from 1501.

SAN TROVASO

Take the Rio Terrà Canal and a bridge to reach the **Campo San Barnaba** ⑫, where the Calle Lunga San Barnaba begins; the first turning to the left, the Calle delle Turchette, connects with the Rio delle Eremite (Romite). This canal comes out in the Rio degli Ognissanti; follow its left-hand side as far as the church of **San Trovaso** ⑫ (open: Mon–Sat 8–11am and 3–6pm), which dates back to the 9th century, though it received its present form from 1584 onwards.

The left transept has a *Last Supper* by Tintoretto (1556) on its right-hand wall; the *Washing of the Feet* opposite is also attributed to him. There is another Tintoretto in the chapel to the left of the high altar: his *Temptation of St Antony* (1577). In the chapel to the right of the high altar is a Gothic painting, *St Chrysogonus on Horseback* by Michele Giambono (15th-century).

LA GIUDECCA

The path beside the canal comes out at the landing-stage of Zattere on the Canale della Giudecca. The south-facing café terraces here are a good place to get an early tan in the spring.

Take a short walk to the next landing-stage, **San Basilio** ⑬; there is a good view of the skyline of Giudecca island along the way. The massive ruined brick building is the Molino Stucky (Stucky Mill), a neo-Gothic flour mill built in 1895 and in operation until the 1950s.

At the landing-stage, take the water-bus across to **Sacca Fisola** ⑬ on the Giudecca, then walk the short distance to the campo. Geometrically laid-out new buildings, all of them very suburban, present another side of Venice altogether. At the landing-stage there are connections to San Marco and Piazzale Roma.

Excursions

San Michele – Murano – Burano – Torcello – Lido – Pellestrina – Chioggia

Map
on page
97

There are more than 40 islands scattered across the Lagoon. Some, like tiny Torcello, colourful Burano and the most famous, Murano, have preserved their autonomy and artistic traditions. Others are now uninhabited, while others still have sunk beneath the surface and exist only as marks on a maritime chart.

SAN MICHELE

The walled island of ★ **San Michele** contains nothing but Venice's cemetery and the oldest Renaissance church in the city. The church of San Michele was designed by Mauro Codussi, and begun in 1469. The vestibule is separated from the rest of the church by the monks' choir, which hides the interior with its ★ **coffered ceiling**. On the left just after you enter is the ★ **Cappella Emiliana** (16th-century). This hexagonal domed

Murano canal front

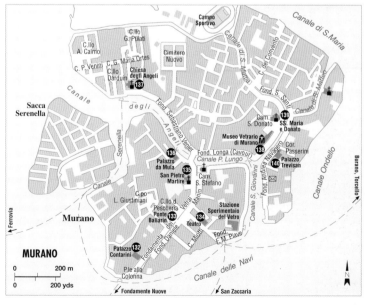

Map on page 97

chapel by Jacopo Sansovino(1560–62) is a masterpiece of Lombardesque marble architecture. The reliefs on the altar include an *Annunciation*, an *Adoration of the Magi* and an *Adoration of the Shepherds* by Antonio da Carona.

The church's characteristic campanile was completed in 1460. The portal with its pointed arch on the right displaying St Michael the dragon-slayer leads into the cloister, which in turn leads to the **cemetery** itself (open: daily 7.30am–4pm). Those buried on this island include the poet Ezra Pound, the Russian impressario Sergei Diaghilev and his composer protégé Igor Stravinsky. The cemetery is now full, and today Venice's dead are laid to rest on the mainland.

Below: Stravinsky's grave
Bottom: San Michele's cloister

MURANO

The island of ★★ **Murano** has been described as a mini-Venice. Like the mother-city, it is made up of islands divided by canals lined by old mansions and palazzi. It even has its own Grand Canal.

Leave the water-bus at Colonna landing-stage. On the Fondamenta dei Vetrai stands the 16th-century Lombardesque **Palazzo Contarini** ⓲. At **Ponte Ballarin** ⓳, proclamations were read next to the column with the symbolic lion; on the other side the Viale Garibaldi leads past the former **Teatro** ⓴ to the lighthouse (Faro). Walk-

ing along the Fondamenta San Giovanni and Colleoni to the Campo Santo Stefano, there are fine views to be had of several magnificent facades. This world-famous island of glass-blowers was known for its prosperity and its generously proportioned palaces and gardens until its decline in the 19th century.

From the campo the bridge leads to the church of **San Pietro Martire** ⓭. Enter via its 16th-century Renaissance portal. On the right wall there are two works by Giovanni Bellini: *Madonna with Angels and Saints*, and *Madonna Enthroned*; on the left are *St Agatha in Prison* and *St Hieronymus in the Wilderness*, both by Veronese. A short distance along on to the left stands the **Palazzo da Mula** ⓰. Though the facade is elaborate Late Gothic, a delightful little ★ wall with Byzantine arches has survived in the garden from the 12th or 13th century (access via the courtyard when the glassworks are open or if there is an exhibition).

GLASS MUSEUM

The Lombardesque **Chiesa degli Angeli** ⓱ can be seen from the canal bridge. The clear lines of its facade are convincing from a distance; close up, the building is in disrepair. After the bridge, the path along the canal leads around the promontory and to the ★ **Museo Vetrario di Murano** ⓲ (open: Thur–Tues 10am–5pm). The former bishop's palace (built 1698) contains over 400 items documenting the history of the famed Venetian glass industry.

VENETIAN GLASS

In 1291 Venice's glassmaking workshops were shifted to Murano because of the danger of fire and possibly industrial espionage. From here, the whole of Europe was supplied with fine glassware and mirrors, until Bohemian glass finally dominated the market in the 18th century. Being a glass-blower in Murano was considered a great honour, and entailed much responsibility: marriage into patrician families was quite normal, and

Star Attraction
● Murano

Buses to the islands
Vaporetto Lines 41 and 42 run from Fondamenta Nuove to San Michele and all landing-stages on Murano. Line 12 goes to Murano, Burano and Torcello. Line 14 connects San Zaccaria with Torcello and Burano via the Lido and Punta Sabbioni.

Murano glass

Map on page 97

Map on page 97

Warning: hard sell
Beware of touts in Piazza San Marco offering 'free' trips to Murano by water-taxi. They are on commission from the glass factories, so you will be herded into a showroom and heavily pressured to buy, at prices often higher than those in Venice. If you choose not to buy anything, they can turn very unpleasant – and may even abandon you on Murano.

revealing trade secrets was punishable by death. Only the craftsmen of Murano understood how to manufacture the thin, colourless glass and then give it its special elaborate designs and colours. The craft is still practised here today (you can watch glassblowing in many of the workshops) although much of the glassware sold in Venice is Far East imitations in the Murano style.

SS MARIA E DONATO

Apart from its glass, Murano's other claim to fame is the basilica of ★★ **SS Maria e Donato** ⑮ (open: daily 9am–noon and 4–7pm) a superb Byzantine building dating from 1140. The simple clarity of line in the nave of this brick building is most impressive. In contrast, the apse, which faces the canal and was originally at the entrance to Murano from the lagoon, possesses a special elegance and beauty of its own: two tiers of arches are supported by thin marble columns, the upper arcade open, the lower one closed. The interior has a wooden ship's keel roof (early 15th-century). The mosaic in the apse dates from the time the church was built, as does the ★★ **mosaic pavement**, with its plant and animal motifs, including two cockerels carrying a dead fox, symbolic of the victory of Christianity over paganism.

Colourful Burano
The path beside the canal now leads from the

campo across the bridge and to the right, to the elegant **Palazzo Trevisan** ⓵⓿, whose neoclassical facade is reminiscent of Palladio and still bears traces of earlier decoration. At the Navagero stop, line 52 connects with Venice via San Michele, or you can get off at Murano's Faro stop to take line 12 to Burano and Torcello.

Star Attractions
● SS Maria e Donato
● Basilica di Santa Maria Assunta

BURANO

The picturesque island village of ★ **Burano**, with its brightly painted houses, is the centre of the Venetian **lace industry**, another very useful source of income for the Venetians from the 16th century onwards. In the main square is the **Scuola dei Merletti** (Lace-making School), which still takes students and has an interesting museum (open: Wed–Mon 9am–5pm). Burano's most famous son was the operatic composer Baldassare Galuppi (1703–85).

Below: Burano lace
Bottom: Santa Maria Assunta open timber roof

TORCELLO

Torcello (founded in the 7th century) was once an important trading centre and had its own bishop. Today the island still trades in fruit and vegetables. The bishop's seat, the ★★ **Basilica di Santa Maria Assunta**, was founded in 639 and consecrated in its present form in 1008. It is the oldest surviving building in the lagoon. Remains of the 7th-century baptistery have been discovered in front of its facade. The south wall of the basilica is the only one with any windows, since no light ever comes from the north and making windows simply for decoration was still unheard of.

The dignified interior (open: daily 10am–5pm) is remarkably spacious, with a superb marble pavement. The aisles are separated by slender marble columns and spanned by an **open timber roof**. The greatest treasures are the 11th-century iconostasis (rood screen), consisting of four large marble panels elaborately carved with Late Byzantine designs, and the ★★ **mosaics** in the presbytery which date back to the 7th century. The fine *Madonna* in the apse, however, is 13th-century,

Map on page 97

The South Lagoon
From San Zaccaria, water-bus Lines 82, 52, 14, 6, 1, and 4 (summer only) connect with the island of Lido – Santa Maria Elisabetta. From there, Line 11 travels to the island of Pellestrina and continues to Chioggia.

Below: a Lido hotel
Bottom: Chioggia beach

and the dramatic *Last Judgement* on the west wall dates from 1190. The tall, square, detached campanile (11th- to 12th-century) is a striking landmark in the lagoon (open: daily 10.20am–5.30pm).

The **Museo dell'Estuario** (open: daily except Mon 10.30am–5pm) contains a collection of Greco-Roman items and archaeological finds from the Estuary from the Paleo-Vento and Etruscan periods. Outside is a primitive stone seat known as Attila's Chair.

LIDO AND PELLESTRINA

The **Lido**, with its fine, sandy beaches, villas, exclusive hotels and many sports facilities, is Venice's international summer health resort. The Film Festival takes place here annually in late August-early September. The water-bus travels via Malamocco, the ancient harbour destroyed by a tidal wave around 1107, and then on to Alberoni on the southern tip of the island. Try to avoid it on Sundays in summer, when all of Venice invades the Lido.

The charming island of **Pellestrina**, with its fishing villages, is ideal for peaceful strolls, and has its own shipbuilding industry near San Pietro in Volta. Pellestrina is protected from the Adriatic by the **murazzi** – mighty embankments over 4km (2½ miles) long and 4.5m (14¾ft) high, completed 1751.

CHIOGGIA

At the southern end of the lagoon, ★ **Chioggia** is a small town on two islands veined with canals. It never really recovered from its destruction during the war with the Genoese (1379–80), but today is one of the main fishing ports on the Adriatic, and a huge market is held here every morning. In summer there are theatre performances and concerts. The smaller island of **Sottomarina** is a beach resort – Chioggia's Lido.

At the Piazzetta Vigo landing-stage the main street, Corso del Popolo, begins beneath a shady series of arcades. The Corso goes past the church of Sant'Andrea on the left (facade 1743) and then the long, one-storeyed granary built in 1322, which survived the destruction of the town by the Genoese. On the canal behind is the famous fish market. At the next left turn off the Corso is the **Chiesa della Trinità**, containing paintings from the Tintoretto and Veronese schools.

CATHEDRAL AND CHURCH

Two churches stand on the Campo del Duomo at the lower end of the Corso. ★**San Martino** (1392), the small brick church with the square apse and octagonal drum, is a rather clumsy Gothic structure and was erected to commemorate the end of the war with Genoa. It contains a ★★**polyptych** with 27 panels (dated 1349) illustrating the *Legend of St Martin*, attributed to Paolo Veneziano. The nearby **Duomo** of Chioggia was rebuilt in the neoclassical style by Baldassare Longhena after a fire in 1623, and construction work stopped in 1674 before the facade was completed. Inside the building, the unusual ★ **vaulted ceiling** of the baroque chapel to the right of the sanctuary with its stucco catches the eye.

On the way back to the landing-stage, a detour from the Corso to admire Chioggia's many fine Gothic and Renaissance facades is highly recommended.

Star Attraction
● **Legend of St Martin polyptych**

Below: fishermen, Chioggia harbour
Bottom: sailing across the Lagoon at dusk

Art and Architecture

Venice's early connection with Byzantium meant that it also came into contact with Byzantine art: Byzantine artists worked in Venice, the local inhabitants learned from them, and several East Roman works of art found their way to the city. This meant that, from the Early Middle Ages onwards, Venetian art developed in distinctly different ways from that of the rest of Europe.

EASTERN INFLUENCES

The domed church of San Marco, begun in 1063 *(see page 21)*, was based on a Byzantine model, and its ground-plan provided the inspiration for several of the churches in the city right up until the 18th century.

Characteristic of Byzantine structures is the high and elegant round arch supported by slender columns with richly decorated capitals: typical examples are Fondaco dei Turchi *(see page 41)*, SS Maria e Donato on Murano, and Santa Fosca on Torcello.

During the mid-12th century, when the powerful Romanesque rounded arch was dominating Central Europe, Venice refused to adopt it – after all, it already had its elegant arches from the East. Romanesque in Venice can only be traced to the architecture of certain campaniles. The state church of San Marco did, however, receive a Romanesque alteration on its facade *(see page 21)*. After all, the city's *nouveaux riches* merchants always wanted the very latest of everything.

THE GOTHIC MIRACLE

Gothic architecture originated in France in the 12th century, but it had lost much of its theological basis by the time it reached the lagoon. The 14th-century Gothic icing that can be seen on San Marco today reveals that it was simply borrowed as a means of decoration. The architecture of the Doge's Palace, however, shows how these borrowed forms gradually blended into Venetian Gothic, a decorative art that transformed the face

Arab inspiration
Venice's contact with North Africa and the Middle East provided the Arab inspiration in Venetian architecture: the Moresco (Moorish) arch became an enchanting window form. Beautifully sculpted Moresco arches decorate the north portal of San Marco, as well as the entrance to its treasury. The East was also the likely origin of the opulent mosaic decoration; the earliest master mosaicists were probably Byzantine émigrés, and some of their best work can be admired on Torcello *(see page 101)*.

Opposite: Scuola Grande de San Giovanni
Below: the Ecstasy of St Mark

of the city. Ogee arches became a Venetian speciality – the Gothic severity from the north thus fell prey to Oriental fantasy and secular curiosity.

The miracle wrought by the advent of the Gothic style can be admired all over the city, in particular on the Doge's Palace as well as several facades along the Canal Grande *(see page 39)*. But the soaring, cathedral-like aspect of Gothic is missing. The few Gothic churches Venice possesses are broad, rather stolid structures – for one thing, the mendicant orders weren't too keen on the expense involved in building, and for another the land posed several foundation problems. Thus the stone vaults that are the golden rule everywhere else are the exception in Venice (SS Giovanni e Paolo). Instead, Venetian ship's carpenters constructed wooden 'ship's keel' roofs – a real Venetian speciality (San Giacomo dell'Orio, San Polo, etc) – and also the wooden beams that were structurally necessary to strengthen the arcades and which actually contain iron chains (the Frari, Santo Stefano, etc).

Below: the Frari exterior
Bottom: the Doge's Palace

RENAISSANCE

The Lombardesque style (its main exponents came from Lombardy) arrived in Venice in the late 15th century, and left behind several superb marble facades and intarsias (Palazzo Dario, *see*

page 46). Very noticeable here are the playful semi-circles that were a particular favourite with the architect Mauro Codussi (San Zaccaria, Scuola di San Marco). He built the Palazzo Vendramin *(see page 41)* with its Tuscan Renaissance windows, and the Palazzo Corner-Spinelli *(see page 44)*, an Early Renaissance jewel.

TUSCAN AND LOMBARDESQUE INFLUENCE

During the High Renaissance the spirit of Rome came to Venice in the shape of architect Jacopo Sansovino. His library building on the Piazzetta *(see page 19)* completes the three main sources of inspiration in Venetian art: San Marco (Byzantium – East), the Doge's Palace (Gothic – North) and the Old Library (Renaissance – West).

Very soon after Sansovino's death in 1570, a classicism, indeed almost a neoclassicism, emerged, but the use of pillars and arches for spatial effect on facades, borrowed from Antiquity, remained obligatory. However, designers no longer wanted to rely on simple imitation, and this new architectural mood resulted in much that was vulgar: the city's buildings started growing extra pillars and whole storeys, and the skyline changed visibly. Buildings appeared which seem grafted on to the cityscape: Ca' Pesaro, Palazzo Labia, the Palazzo Grimani, Ca' Rezzonico, the Palazzo Grassi, Ca' Grande and the Palazzo Pisano are all variations on the same theme created over a period of 200 years.

The prolific ornamentation on the church of Santa Maria della Salute (consecrated 1687) by Baldassare Longhena is almost a symbol of this exhaustion of formal language. Venice, deprived of its role as a world trading power, was putting up a facade to hide its loss of face.

VENETIAN BAROQUE?

Several sacred and secular buildings appeared in Venice during the baroque era without actually being baroque structures. The style, which originated in Rome in around 1600 and took roughly

> **Palladio in Venice**
> The Renaissance architect Palladio (1508–80), from Vicenza, was unable to realise his monumental temple architecture in Venice, and so he altered his ideal of the Classical facade very constructively, in a geometrical manner: the churches of San Giorgio Maggiore, San Francesco della Vigna, Redentore and Le Zitelle are all masterpieces of harmony and clarity, which is sometimes reiterated in the interiors, such as San Giorgio Maggiore and the superb presbytery in the Redentore.

San Giorgio Maggiore interior

a century to inspire countries north of the Alps, never caught on in Venice. Venice does not actually possess a single baroque building, although several neoclassical facades overloaded with decoration are sometimes confused with the style, (San Moisè, San Stae, Santa Maria del Giglio).

Bellini's 'Madonna and Child'
Bottom: Giorgione's 'The Tempest'

PAINTING

The connection with Byzantium and Orthodox severity meant that Venice hardly noticed the changes taking place in painting in Italy. The developments in Florence and Siena, and even the revolutionary work of Giotto in nearby Padua, were ignored for years. But the construction of the new Doge's Palace changed all that. Talented artists were brought into the city in the first half of the 15th century; they included Gentile da Fabriano from Umbria, and Pisanello, Paolo Uccello and Andrea del Castagno from Tuscany.

The main source of inspiration for Venetian painting was probably Andrea Mantegna (1431–1506), who married into the Bellini family of painters; he taught his father-in-law Jacopo (1400–71) and Jacopo's sons Gentile (1429–1507) and Giovanni (1430–1516), about the main achievements of the Renaissance: liberation from medieval formalism, and the introduction of perspective.

The new realism then brought Antonello da Messina (1430–79) to Venice, and oil-painting came with him. He influenced the city's other great painting family, the Vivarini from Murano: Antonio (1415–76), Bartolomeo (1432–99) and Alvise (1446–1505). Both these families made Venetian painting so famous that even Albrecht Dürer was attracted to the lagoon in 1505 to learn from it.

THE GOLDEN AGE OF VENETIAN ART

The heirs to this legacy were the narrative painters Vittore Carpaccio (1486–1525) and Giorgione (1478–1510), who stood on the threshold of the triumphant 16th century, and were duly followed by the great master artists Titian (*circa*

1488–1576), Tintoretto (1518–94) and Paolo Veronese (1528–88).

Painting had finally been freed from its medieval straitjacket, but each of these three artists used the space thus gained in a subjective way: Titian perfected the use of colour, and his work is distinctive for its humanity; Veronese, with his serene skies, is optimistic and worldly; and the expressive dramas of Tintoretto are full of searching questions: light, space and movement transcend the actual subjects of his work. He had a great effect on his most famous pupil, El Greco (Domenico Theotocopoulos, originally from Crete).

After this high point of Venetian painting, Palma il Giovane (1544–1628) was still able to regard himself as the main exponent of the school until numerous imitators exploited the various painting methods. Originality finally returned only in the 18th century: painters Pietro Longhi (1702–85) and Francesco Guardi (1712–93) became chroniclers of Venetian life, while Antonio Canale (better known as Canaletto) became world-famous for his *vedute*, not only of his native city but of several others as well.

The names Giovanni Battista Piazzetta (1682–1754) and Giovanni Battista Tiepolo (1696–1770) also belong at the latter end of the great era of Venetian painting. Piazzetta's pictures

Perfect precision

Canaletto (Antonio Canale, 1697–1768) is famous worldwide for his painstaking, almost photographic views of Venice. A leading light of the *vedutisti* (landscape artists), he took his inspiration in Rome from Gaspar van Wittel and Gian Paolo Pannini, both highly skilled in this genre. Canaletto, who was originally a theatre and opera set painter, had a precise eye for detail. He was much admired by the English aristocracy, and was supported by the collector Joseph Smith, who was at one time British Consul in Venice. Canaletto's views of Venice were such collectable items that very few remain in the city of his inspiration.

Tintoretto's 'Flight into Egypt'

are more sombre and dramatic, while Tiepolo's luminous, poetic frescoes continue the tradition established by Paolo Veronese.

SCULPTURE

Byzantine severity dominated here, too, the only exception being the masterly sculpture for the middle portals of San Marco executed by Benedetto Antelami from Parma, when the basilica was given its Romanesque facade in the 13th century.

Below: the Colleoni statue
Bottom: the Lion of St Mark, the Doge's Palace

It was the large-scale project for the Doge's Palace in the 14th and 15th centuries that really got Venetian sculpture going: the two families of Bon and Delle Masegne worked together as architects-cum-sculptors on the Doge's Palace/ San Marco complex. The large window on the lagoon side of the Doge's Palace and the iconostasis in San Marco are by the Delle Masegne family, while the Ca' d'Oro and the Porta della Carta of the Doge's Palace are by the Bon family. All are masterpieces of Gothic sculpture.

The early Renaissance was distinguished by the skills of the Lombardo family of architects: Pietro (1435–1515) and his sons Tullio (*circa* 1455–1532) and Antonio (c 1458–1516) built tombs and did much intarsia work for Venice's illustrious elite (SS Giovanni e Paolo, Santa Maria dei

Miracoli, San Giobbe, sculptures on the choir screens in the Frari). The imposing equestrian statue of Colleoni on the Campo SS Giovanni e Paolo was designed by Andrea Verrocchio (1436–88), and the marvellous statues of Adam and Eve on the Arco Foscari (interior courtyard of the Doge's Palace) are by Antonio Rizzo, who built the neighbouring Scala dei Giganti.

Sculpture in Venice reached its high point with *Mars and Neptune* by the great Jacopo Sansovino (1486–1570), who also designed the Loggetta. He was assisted in his work on the Old Library and the Scala d'Oro (Doge's Palace) by Alessandro Vittoria (1524–1608).

The years that followed produced only undistinguished descendants of the great masters.

Music and Theatre

In 1527, the Flemish composer Adriaan Willaert (1480–1562) was appointed *maestro di cappella* of St Mark's. During his 35 years in the post Venice became the centre of western European music. He developed a style of polyphony in which two four-part choirs sang alternately, and this became characteristic of the Venetian school under his successors, Andrea Gabrieli (*circa* 1510–86) and Giovanni Gabrieli (1557–1612).

Another famous music director of St Mark's was Claudio Monteverdi (1567–1643), the founder of opera in its present form. By 1678 there were already seven opera houses (alongside 11 theatres that staged performances daily). Among the better-known exponents of Venetian opera were Francesco Cavalli (1602–76) and Marcantonio Cesti (1623–69). Venice's last great native composer was Antonio Vivaldi (1669–1741), who taught music at the girls' orphanage at Santa Maria della Pietà.

THEATRE

The Goldoni Theatre puts on works by Venice's most celebrated playwright, Carlo Goldoni, as well as classic plays in Italian, while the Teatro

Commedia dell'Arte
The style of improvised ensemble theatre known as Commedia dell'Arte originated in Venice: the characters Arlecchino (Harlequin) and Brighella articulated popular sentiment in their never-ending struggle with Pantalone (Pantaloon), the merchant, and Balanzone, the doctor. The genre crystallised into a series of improvisations on stock situations until Carlo Goldoni (1707–93) created a new and more realistic form of Italian comedy. He held a mirror up to his country — and was exiled for his pains.

Pantalone the merchant

Al'Avogaria is a tiny theatre performing *Commedia dell'Arte*-style plays.

Before the disastrous fire of 1996, the Gran Teatro La Fenice hosted opera, ballet and concerts from October to July. First built in 1792, it staged various premières including Rossini's *Tancredi* (1813), Verdi's *Rigoletto* (1851) and *La Traviata* (1853) and Stravinsky's *The Rake's Progress* (1951). Since the 1996 fire, performances have been held at the Pala Fenice on Tronchetto (tel: 041 520 5422). There is a temporary box office beside the Cassa di Risparmio bank in Campo San Luca, open 8.30am–1pm (tel: 041 521 0161).

Below: 'The Ballet Master' by Pietro Longhi
Bottom: carnival masks

CONCERTS

Music of all kinds, from ancient to contemporary, is performed in the magnificent rooms of the city's churches and palazzi: the organ concerts in San Marco, San Giorgio Maggiore and Santa Maria della Pietà are very highly regarded. Chamber music, baroque and Venetian music are often performed at the Ateneo San Basso (Piazzetta dei Leoni), at the Scuola Grande di San Rocco in summer and at the Ateneo Veneto (Campo di San Fantin) in winter. At the Teatro Fondamente Nuove (near the church of the Gesuiti) you can listen to experimental and contemporary music.

Festivals in Venice

The Biennale takes place in odd-numbered years from June to September/October. Although its official role is as an art exhibition (in the Giardini Pubblici since 1895), it also includes exhibitions of architecture and photography, as well as performances of theatre and music (Magazzini, Corderie, around the harbour and on the Giudecca).

International Film Festival is held annually at the Lido from August to September. During this time, and in July too, movies (often in the original language) are also shown in the open-air Cinema all'Aperto in Campo San Polo.

Carnivale: This takes place 12 days before Ash Wednesday, and takes over the whole town –

masked balls, a huge programme of events, and the city suddenly becomes a theatre.

There are also several festivals that date from the city's days as a world sea-power:

Festa della Sensa (Ascension): On the Sunday after Ascension Day, celebrating the marriage of Venice with the sea.

Vogalonga: On a Sunday in May everything remotely seaworthy is hauled out for this huge rowing festival (*Vogalonga* means 'long row'). The route from the Giudecca Canal to Burano and back to San Marco is around 30km (19 miles).

Festa del Redentore: On the third weekend in July a bridge of boats is constructed across the Giudecca Canal to the Redentore, the church built in gratitude for deliverance of the city from the plague of 1576. Boats are magnificently adorned and there is a fireworks display on the Saturday night.

Regata Storica: On the first Sunday in September this regatta, which features historical ships and costumes, is held in the Canal Grande.

Festa della Salute: In the second half of November a bridge of boats is constructed across the Canal Grande close to the Gritti Palace Hotel; on 21 November the procession leads from the church of Santa Maria delle Salute (built in thanksgiving for the city's escape from the plague of 1630) to San Marco and back.

> **The Venice Carnival**
>
> Carnivale (literally 'farewell to meat') is the extraordinary pre-Lenten pageant that has been celebrated in Venice for centuries – with a few temporary interruptions. It was forbidden by Napoleon in 1797, and again by Mussolini, who banned the wearing of masks. The mask tradition allowed the nobility to mingle freely with the lower echelons, and allowed everyone to behave licentiously with anonymity. By the 18th century, Carnivale had grown into a two-month party on the grandest scale. After the constraints imposed by Mussolini, the tradition was not revived until 1979, and today is a somewhat tamer affair. Even so, the whole city manages to take part in the spectacular 10-day celebrations.

Culture fatigue

FOOD AND DRINK

Gastronomically, Venice is the most expensive city in Italy apart from Milan. The fare served by restaurants and *trattorie* here is usually not worth the price charged. Venetian cuisine can be superb – but finding it, at a reasonable price, is an art in itself.

EATING OUT

Broadly speaking, there are three different types of eating-places to choose from. The *osteria* has a limited menu but often offers the best-value meals. (Some, *bacari*, are more like bars serving *cichetti*, the Venetian equivalent of *tapas*.) The *trattoria* tends to be a cheaper version of a restaurant, usually family-run with good home cooking. The *ristorante* is usually smarter and more expensive – although many places that are really *trattorie* call themselves restaurants, and vice versa.

Rosticcerie are self-service establishments, with cheaper prices and usually satisfactory food. The menus feature some Venetian dishes, too. Pizza is also available everywhere, in every variation. But do not expect the quality of central or southern Italy here, as there are no wood-burning ovens.

Some bars in Venice offer all kinds of delicious foods that can be enjoyed on small plates accompanied by a glass of wine: every kind of seafood, served with steamed vegetables and *polenta*. Several *padroni* (bar-keepers) specialise in amazing sandwiches containing mushrooms, tuna, ham, egg, cheese and salad between layers of various types of bread.

VENETIAN CUISINE

Most restaurants specialise in fish, and the range of specialities is vast, from

Opposite: St Mark's Square waiter

anguilla (eel) to *zuppa di pesce* (fish soup). It is worth investing in a *grigliata mista* (mixed seafood grill) at least once. Connoisseurs adore the *risotto di pesce* (fish risotto) and will go out of their way to eat *granseola* (crabmeat with oil and lemon served in a shell). It takes a while to adjust to *bigoli in salsa* (black noodles) and *risotto nero* (black rice); the black colour comes from squid's ink.

Seppie alla veneziana (squid with polenta) combined with *sarde in saor* (fried sardines marinated in vinegar, onions, raisins and pinenuts) is a classic Venetian dish. But fish is the main fare here; the only really popular meat dishes in Venice are *fegato alla veneziana* (calf's liver with onion) and *carpaccio* (thin slices of marinaded beef, invented in Harry's Bar).

VENETIAN WINES

Wines served by the carafe or glass *(vino sfuso)* include Tokai or Soave (white) and Merlot and Cabernet (red). An additional *del Piave* on the label makes the latter two far nobler: the wine-growing area around the Piave

---

Aperitivo
Between six and eight in the evening, when the Venetians crowd the city's bars, a favourite drink is white wine with Campari or Aperol and a dash of soda, known as *spritz* (the word dates back to the Austrian occupation). Another popular *aperitivo* is a glass of Prosecco (here called Prosecchino) or Cartizze, either plain or with a dash of strawberry, pineapple or blackcurrant cordial. The traditional, but less stylish *ombra* (plain white wine) still survives in the San Marco neighbourhood. The evening *aperitivo* may be accompanied by delicious bar snacks (*cicchetti*).

river produces several full-bodied reds. Anyone keen on getting to know the wines of the Veneto well should look for a *cantina* and do some detailed wine-tasting. Good whites – with fine variations in flavour – include the following: Pinot Bianco, Pinot Grigio, Sauvignon and Prosecco, the region's much-loved sparkling wine. Fruity reds include Raboso, Refosco and Marzemino.

Restaurant selection

This is a small selection of the eating-places in Venice, in three categories, according to price: $$$ = expensive; $$ = moderate; $ = inexpensive.

Ai Gondolieri, Ponte del Formager, San Vio, Dorsoduro, tel: 041- 528 6396. Delicious and costly Venetian cuisine, catering especially to carnivores and vegetarians. Good game in season. Closed Tuesday. $$$.

Hotel Cipriani, Giudecca 10, tel: 041-520 7744. Legendary hotel and restaurant, where fish is the speciality. Smart attire required for this gourmet experience. Private boat service from San Marco across to Giudecca. $$$.

Danieli Terrace, Riva degli Schiavoni, 4196 Castello, tel: 041-522 6480. A top-class restaurant with an enchanting view of the lagoon from the fourth floor of the Danieli Hotel. $$$.

Favorita, Via Francesco Duodo, 33 San Nicolo, Lido, tel: 041-526 1626. One of the best restaurants on the Lido and well worth the journey. Seafood is the speciality. Two dining rooms and outdoor seating. $$$.

Caffè Florian, Piazza San Marco, 56 San Marco, tel: 041-528 5338. Founded in 1720, this famous cafe was frequented by Goethe, Mark Twain, Thomas Mann and Ernest Hemingway. The bar inside has intimate wooden booths, and is much cheaper than the tables outside on the piazza. $$$.

Gritti Palace, Campo Santa Maria del Giglio, 2467 San Marco, tel: 041-520 7744. Old recipes from the splendid days of the doges. $$$.

Locanda Cipriani, Piazza Santa Fosca, 29 Torcello, tel: 041-730 150. Despite an almost rural setting on the island of Torcello, prices are big-city high, but ingredients are fresh, dishes refined and service superb. Exceptional views from the terrace. $$$.

Quadri, Piazza San Marco, 120 San Marco, tel: 041-528 9299. Located above the Gran Caffè Quadri (a younger rival to Florian), an elegant restaurant serving high-quality food and superb views over the piazza. $$$.

A good selection of fresh produce

Harry's Bar
The most famous bar in Venice (Calle Vallaresso, 1232 San Marco, tel: 041-528 5777) is the birthplace of the Bellini (Prosecco and white peach juice) and the place where Ernest Hemingway legendarily devised his own cocktail – 1 part Martini to 15 parts gin. The cuisine is among the best in Venice, particularly the pasta and the *carpaccio*, which was invented here. It is considered more chic to dine in the simpler downstairs bar. $$$.

Antica Locanda Montin, Fondamenta Borgo, 1147 Dorsoduro, tel: 041-522 7151. Welcoming restaurant with good service and some seating in the garden courtyard. International/Italian cooking. $$.
Le Bistrot de Venise, Calle dei Fabbri, 4685 San Marco, tel: 041-523 6651. Atmospheric French-style bistro serving Venetian recipes, pizza and French dishes. $$.
Corte Sconta, Calle del Pestrin, 3886 Castello, tel: 041-522 7024. Lively fish restaurant – look for the catch of the day. $$.
Fiaschetteria Toscana, Salizzada San Giovanni Crisostomo, Rialto, tel: 041-528 5281. Despite the name, not a Tuscan restaurant but among the city's best for Venetian specialities. Excellent home-made puddings. $$.
Gam-Gam, Sotto Portego del Ghetto Vecchio, 1122 Cannaregio, tel: 041-715 284. Jewish/kosher cuisine on the edge of the Ghetto. Friendly service. Some tables overlook the canal. $$.
Da Ivo, Calle dei Fuseri, 1809 San Marco, tel: 041-528 5004. A successful marriage of Tuscan and Venetian cuisine in a welcoming ambience. $$.
Taverna La Fenice, Campiello della Fenice, 1938 SanMarco, tel: 041-522 3856. Famous old restaurant (since 1907) beside the site of La Fenice. Pasta, fresh seafood, Venetian specialities. $$.

Fiore, Santo Stefano, 3461 San Marco, tel: 041-523 5310. Simple family-run *trattoria*; classic Venetian dishes include seafood, polenta and risotto. *Cichetti* served at the bar. $$.
Dalle Zanze, Fondamenta Tolentini, 231 Santa Croce, tel: 041-522 3555. Well-established restaurant close to the Grand Canal, specialising in seafood. Very popular: reservations essential. $$.
Al Bottegon, Fondamenta Nanim 992 Dorsoduro, tel: 041-523 0034. Old-fashioned wine-shop-cum-bar (also known as Gia Shiavone), very popular with locals, students and tourists. Freshly made *panini* (open sandwiches), cold meats and cheese. $.
Al Nono Risorto, Calle delle Regina, 2337 Santa Croce, tel: 041-524 1169. Lively pizzeria that also serves Venetian dishes. Attractive garden with shady trees. $.
Paradiso Perduto, Fondamenta della Misericordia, 2540 Cannaregio, tel: 041-720 581. An atmospheric bar/restaurant with outside tables. One of the first places to stay open late in Venice. $.
Da Renato, Rio Tera Secondo, 2245/A San Polo, tel: 041-524 1922. Simple, good Venetian home-cooking in a charming atmosphere. Owner Renato both cooks and offers a warm welcome. $.
Alle Testiere, Calle del Mondo Novo, 5801 Castello, tel: 041-522 7220. Small, very popular *trattoria* serving seafood and Venetian cuisine. Two sittings for dinner (7pm and 9pm): reservations essential. $.
Ai Vecio Fritoin, Calle della Regina, 2262 Santa Croce, tel: 041-522 2881. Preserves the tradition of the *fritoin* – street stall serving the Venetian version of fish and chips. Order fried fish or seafood wrapped in paper to take away (*frito en scartoso*) or enjoy a full meal or bar snack. $.

SHOPPING

Venetian craftsmanship continues to flourish. You don't have to look far to find fascinating specialist shops and local artisans at work in their ateliers. Look out for beautifully crafted Venetian masks, marbled paper, Murano glass, handmade picture frames, lace, linen and jewellery.

The arcades of Piazza San Marco shelter luxury jewellers, hand-embroidered linen and lace, and priceless pieces of glass. The Mercerie ('Haberdashers'), which links Piazza San Marco with the Rialto, is still a busy shopping thoroughfare. Best buys in the area are silk ties; leather goods (mostly made on the nearby Brenta Riviera), especially soft leather wallets; lamb's-wool and angora sweaters. In the Ruga degli Orefici (Street of the Goldsmiths), jewellers have been around for centuries.

ARTS AND CRAFTS

To see authentic Venetian crafts visit **Veneziartigiana** at 412–413 Calle Larga San Marco, just north of the Basilica. This is a fine old apothecary shop converted into a showroom for crafts designed in glass, silver, bronze, china, lace and gold. **Jesurum** on Piazza San Marco and Merceria del Capitello, 4857 San Marco, is a long-established name in lace and linen, while **Trois** on Campo San Maurizio sells fine silks and exotic hand-printed fabrics, including Fortuny-inspired designs. **Gaggio** on Campo Santo Stefano is renowned for printing Art Deco designs on silk and velvet, and **Luigi Bevilacqua**, on Campiello della Comare, Santa Croce, is the other place for hand-crafted fabrics.

The city has a splendid choice of masks, and some of the most eye-catching can be found at **Tragicomica**, Campiello dei Meloni, 1414 San Polo, **Laboratorio Artigiano Maschere**, Barbaria delle Tole, 6657 Castello, **Mondo Novo** at Rio Terrà Canal, Santa Margherita, 3063 Dorsoduro, and **Ca' Macana** at Calle de le Botteghe, San Barnaba, 3172 Dorsoduro.

For hand-printed paper with marble designs and other fine stationery, visit **Legatoria Piazzesi**, Campiello della Feltrina, 2551/C San Marco. You can see the antique woodblocks that are still used to make the paper by the traditional *carta varese* method.

FASHION

The Calle Larga XXII Marzo and the streets between here and Piazza San Marco are the smartest shopping addresses in town. The Salizzada San Moisè boasts big names in shoes, bags and fashions, including Valentino, Versace, Fratelli Rossetti and Louis Vuitton. Slightly more off-beat and fun is the street called **Frezzeria** running north of the Salizzada San Moisè, while **Fiorella** in the Campo Santo Stefano is renowned for the most outlandish fashions.

Venetian Glass

Glass has been made in Venice for centuries, and the items for sale range from tiny glass insects to vast chandeliers. The best choice is found on the glass-making island of Murano where there are many shops and showrooms. Some of the manufacturers also have outlets in Venice. **Venini**, Piazzetta dei Leoni (close to Piazza San Marco) is one of the most reputable firms, making vases, chandeliers, lamps and even witty glass versions of traditional masks. To watch the whole process of glassmaking, visit the Venini factory in Murano (Fondamenta Ventrai 50, tel: 041-739 955).

PRACTICAL INFORMATION

Getting There

BY PLANE

British Airways and Alitalia operate direct flights from London Heathrow to Venice. Many charter operators, and the budget airlines Go and RyanAir, fly from the UK to Treviso, 30km (20 miles) north of Venice. There are no direct flights to Venice from the US.

Marco Polo airport is 9km (5½miles) north of Venice in Tessera near Mestre (*see Map, page 8,* tel: 041-260 9260). To get to the city takes 30 minutes by a bus that runs as far as the Piazzale Roma (buy tickets from the ATVO office in the arrival area or on board the bus when office is closed), or 45 minutes by the more romantic *motoscafo* (motor-boat) to San Marco, via Murano and the Lido. Treviso airport is connected to Venice by public buses and a frequent train service.

BY RAIL

Venice is connected with the international rail network by the main station of Santa Lucia. Arriving by train you have the advantage of an information office within the station, more porters available and a wide choice of water transport below the station.

BY CAR

Driving into Venice is best avoided. Garaging costs are high and space at Piazzale Roma for most of the year is non-existent. This means parking outside Venice, either at Tronchetto (a parking island) or Fusina, found at the mouth of the Brenta Canal.

Visitors from the north will approach either from Austria or Switzerland. The main traffic routes are as follows:

● Innsbruck over the Brenner Pass, Bolzano, Trento, Verona, Padua, Venice. All on the motorway.
● Innsbruck over the Brenner Pass, Bolzano, Trento, Bassano, Venice. Motorway as far as Trento.
● From Zürich over the St Gotthard Pass, then through Milan, Bergamo, Verona, Padua, Venice. Partly motorway in Switzerland, all motorway in Italy. There are toll charges on all motorways in Italy.

A driving licence and vehicle registration documents, a warning triangle and country stickers are compulsory. The international green insurance card doesn't have to be shown at the border but is advisable in case of accident. Comprehensive cover is recommended.

The maximum speed allowed on Italy's toll motorways is 130kmph (80mph) for cars with capacities of over 1.1 litres; smaller vehicles may not travel faster than 110kmph (68mph); and the usual limit on country roads is 90kmph (56mph). Seat belts are compulsory in Italy.

Getting Around

PARKING

Piazzale Roma (the most central car park) is connected to San Marco and the Lido by water-bus Lines 1, 52, 82, N (night) and 4 (summer only). Line 82 connects the car park on the island of Tronchetto with San Marco and the Lido. In the peak season between June and September there are also extra car parks at Fusina and San Giuliano; line 16 serves Fusina–Zattere year-round.

WATER-BUSES

The most important *vaporetto* (water-bus) connections all link with the

Piazzale Roma, where all land vehicles have to turn back. Buy tickets at the small kiosk. Large baggage costs extra, although one item of hand-luggage is included in the cheaper 24-hour, 3-day and 7-day tickets. Tickets must be stamped by the machine alongside the landing-stage before boarding.

Line 1 operates the whole year round along the Canal Grande from Tronchetto to Lido. It is supplemented by line 82 as far as San Zaccaria (and to the Lido in season), but the latter line does not stop everywhere. The section in the Canal Grande is described in Route 2 *(see page 39)*.

Lines 51 and 52 take a circular route around the city centre in both directions (*circolare destra* round to the right, or clockwise, *circolare sinistra* anticlockwise) and are ideal for a city round trip. Line 3 is a seasonal route from Tronchetto down the Grand Canal to San Zaccaria and returning via the Giudecca Canal. Line 4 is the reverse of Line 3, starting at San Zaccaria, but passing the Lido on the way back.

Lines 41 and 42 provide the only water-borne route through the Arsenale and boatyard area. The lines that operate to the northern and southern parts of the lagoon are described in the *Excursions* section *(see page 97)*. There is also a year-round direct con-nection with Chioggia from the Piazzale Roma. Line 14 operates all year round from Riva Schiavoni via Lido to Punta Sabbioni, where there is a bus connection to Jesolo. Both Punta Sabbioni and Lido are served by the Line 17 car ferry, which operates the whole year round from Tronchetto.

The main lines run non-stop, but there are fewer boats at night – time-tables are posted at all landing-stages and are available at the ACTV offices at Ponte dei Fuseri and at Piazzale Roma (ACTV tel: 041-528 7886 or 041-272 2111).

Water Taxis

These smart, varnished launches all have meters and must display a list of charges and a map of the city. There are taxi 'ranks' at San Marco, Piazzale Roma, Rialto and other main points in the city, otherwise call 041-523 5775 or 041-522 2303. There is a minimum fare to cover the first 7 minutes, then a lower payment for each additional minute.

Venice and its Gondolas

The gondolas have been black only since 1562, when they became so over-ornate (due to the city's wealthy families' continuous attempts to upstage one another) that a law was passed. As a means of transport, though, they have been in use ever since the time of the first doges (697).

A gondola is 10.15m (33⅓ft) long and 1.40m (4.6ft) wide, and also 24cm (9.5 inches) shorter on their right-hand side – a peculiarity explained by the fact that the gondolier only places his pole in the water on the right in order to steer. The prow is decorated with a curious toothed projection called the *ferro*, with six strips that are meant to symbolise the six *sestieri* (districts) into which Venice was divided in 1169. The seventh one, pointing in

Water rates

The price of a gondola ride is fixed by law. As of April 2001, the daytime fare is €60 for the first 50 minutes and €30 for each additional 25 minutes. At night (8pm– 8am) these rates rise to €80 and €40 respectively. Most gondolas carry up to six people. It is sensible to agree in advance with your gondolier where you want to be taken and how long you expect the journey to take.

another direction, stands for the island of Giudecca, and the round part is meant to portray the doge's hat.

Along certain parts of the Canal Grande the gondola still functions as a *traghetto* (ferry) from one bank to the other. Operating between Rialto fish market (Pescheria) and Strada Nuova (Ca' d'Oro), S. Maria del Giglio and Salute, and S. Tomá and Ca' Garzoni (near Palazzo Grassi), they are a great way to save walking and only cost around €0.30 (for Venetians as well as tourists).

The city's 400 private gondolas are mainly used by visitors eager to discover the city's canals but, with or without music, during the day or during a romantic evening, Venice wouldn't be the same without a gondola ride.

TO PADUA ON THE 'BURCHIELLO'

Today's *Burchiello* motor-launch is only related in name to the historic ship that used to take a day to reach Padua via the Brenta Canal two centuries ago. The trip includes a visit to some of the magnificent villas lining the banks of the canal (e.g. Villa Malcontenta by Palladio, Villa Nazionale in Stra). The service operates from April through to October three days a week (usually Tuesday, Thursday and Saturday).

Facts for the Visitor
TRAVEL DOCUMENTS
Visitors from the EU, Commonwealth countries and the US need only a passport for a stay of up to three months. Citizens of other countries should check with the nearest Italian consulate about visas before travelling.

CUSTOMS
You're allowed to bring in as much currency as you like. Non-EU citizens can bring 400 cigarettes, one bottle of spirits, two of wine and 50g of perfume. EU citizens no longer have to declare goods. Non-EU citizens can claim back VAT (IVA). Look out for shops saying *Tax free for tourists.*

Unlimited amounts of foreign currency and euros may be brought in and out of Italy, but need to be declared if the sum exceeds €10,500.

TOURIST INFORMATION
Information can be obtained from the Italian State Tourist Offices (ENIT) at the following addresses:
In the UK: Italian State Tourist Office, 1 Princes Street, London W1, tel: 020-7408 1254; fax: 020-7493 6695; website: www.enit.it/uk

Telephoning al fresco

In the US: Italian Government Tourist Office, 630 5th Avenue, Suite 1565, NY 10111, New York, tel: 212 245 4822; fax: 212 586 9249; website: www.italiantourism.com

In Venice: Piazza San Marco, 71/F (Ala Napoleonica), tel: 041 529 8711; fax: 041 523 0399; APT Venice Pavilion, Giardini Ex Reali, San Marco; the railway station; Piazzale Roma (car park); Lido, Gran Viale 6. Hotel receptions can provide the free brochure, *Un Ospite di Venezia* (*Guest in Venice*), published monthly in Italian and English. *Venice Pocket*, a free quarterly publication in English, can be obtained from the tourist office; or you can buy *Venice News* from a newsstand.

Assistance on call

The ATP has set up a 24-hour tourist helpline called 'Venezia No Problem'. If you have difficulties, or encounter poor service or 'behaviour contrary to the rights of the tourist' – for instance bad service from hotels, restaurants, water taxis, etc – you should call the toll-free number 800 355 920.

ROLLING VENICE CARD

Young people between 14 and 30 years of age can obtain this pass for a small fee from the Agenzia Transalpino at the railway station. It provides several discounts and comes with a variety of useful booklets on itineraries, sightseeing, cheap accommodation and restaurants. Don't forget to bring a passport-sized photo plus passport.

CURRENCY

In February 2002, the euro (EUR) became the official currency used in Italy, along with most other member states of the European Union. Euro notes are denominated in 5, 10, 20, 50,

100 and 500 euros; coins in 1 and 2 euros and 1, 2, 5, 10, 20 and 50 cents.

BANKS AND EXCHANGE

Bank hours vary, but are generally Monday to Friday 8.30am–1.20pm and one hour in the afternoon from 2.30–3.30pm, but check locally as afternoon opening times vary. Banks close on weekends and holidays. The *bureaux de change* are open during shopping hours. The exchange offices at the airport and railway station open until the evenings and at weekends.

Traveller's cheques and cheques can be changed at most hotels. Exchange rates vary but banks rates are usually the most favourable. Using an international debit or credit card at the automated 'Bancomat' cash dispensers found at most banks brings the lowest rate.

BILLS

Restaurants, shops and other establishments are required by law (for tax reasons) to issue an official receipt to customers, who should not leave the premises without it.

TIPPING

Even though service is now officially included everywhere, tipping is still customary and bills are rounded up.

OPENING TIMES

Most fashion and tourist shops are open from 9am to 7.30pm. In other shops there is generally a lunch break from 12.30 or 1pm to 3 or 3.30pm. Food shops are open 8am–1pm and 5–7.30pm. Saturday is an ordinary working day; some shops close on Monday morning or Wednesday afternoon.

POST

The main post office is close to the Rialto Bridge in the Fondaco dei Tedeschi. It is open Monday to Saturday 9am–6.45pm, Sunday 9am–

noon. Other post offices, including one just west of Piazza San Marco in the Calle Larga dell'Ascensione, are open Monday to Friday 8.30am–1.30pm. Stamps *(francobolli)* can be purchased from post offices and also from tobacconists *(tabacchi)*.

TELEPHONING

This can be done from public telephones, either with *gettoni* (phone tokens) or with 100-, 200- and 500-lire coins. Phone cards *(carta telefonica)* are also available for €2.50, €5 or €7.50 at tobacconists and newsstands. There are public phones at the main post office (open 24 hours). International dialling codes: Australia 61; UK 44; US and Canada 1. To call Venice, even from within the city, you must always dial the area code 041; if calling from abroad, the '0' is retained.

TIME

Italy is six hours ahead of US Eastern Standard Time and one hour ahead of Greenwich Mean Time.

ELECTRICITY

Usually 220v, occasionally 110v. Safety plugs cannot always be used. Specialist shops can provide adaptors.

PUBLIC HOLIDAYS

1 January, 6 January, 25 April, 1 May, 15 August, 1 November, 21 November, 8 December, 25–26 December, Good Friday, Easter Monday. If a public holiday happens to fall on a Tuesday or Thursday, the intervening Monday or Friday may also be taken as a holiday.

MEDICAL

Visitors from the EU have the right to claim health services available to Italians. UK visitors should obtain Form E111 from a post office before departure, but private insurance is also recommended

---

Visiting the sights
Restoration work is common and some churches and palazzi have been closed for many years. Projected re-opening dates are usually optimistic, although there are always exceptions. The opening hours cited here are likely to change without warning. To avoid disappointment, check on the opening of particular sights before you visit. Note that photography is not usually permitted in churches or museums.

There is a 24-hour casualty department at Ospedale Civile, Campo dei SS Giovanni e Paolo, tel: 041-523 0000. Local newspapers and the booklet *Un Ospite di Venezia* list late-night chemists. A late-night rota is also shown on the door of every pharmacy.

THEFT AND OTHER EMERGENCIES

Venice is one of the safest cities in Europe but you should nevertheless watch your valuables in crowded places, especially on the *vaporetti*. It is best to leave valuables in the hotel safe and carry money on your person rather than in a shoulder-bag or handbag.

In case of theft head immediately to the police *(Questura)* to make an official declaration. A lost passport should be reported to your consulate.
Medical emergency, tel: 118
All emergencies, tel: 113
Police emergency, tel: 112
Police general, San Marco 996 (off Calle dei Fabri), tel: 041-522 5434.

LOST AND FOUND

Lost property offices *(uffici oggetti rinvenuti)* are in the Town Hall, Palazzo Loredan, Riva del Carbon, San Marco (Monday to Friday 8am–2pm); at the station (daily 8am–noon and 3–6pm); at the ACTV office, Piazzale Roma, daily 7.30am–12.30pm or tel: 041-528 7886.

ACCOMMODATION

Venice is one of those cities that always has tourists staying, whatever the time of year, and the accommodation situation has developed to cope with this. Timely booking is still advisable, though, especially for the summer season, Easter, Whitsun, Carnival and during the Biennale or Film Festival *(see page 112)*.

In Venice, the difference between luxury accom- modation and the simple *locanda* (boarding-house) is the same as everywhere else. Simpler places can entail some surprises, some pleasant, some not so pleasant. It's always a good idea to take a look at the room first. Nothing is cheap in Venice, and that includes accommodation; staying on the mainland will save you a great deal of money.

HOTELS IN VENICE

Hotels *(alberghi)* in Venice are officially classed into five categories: luxury hotels $$$$$; category I $$$$; category II $$$; category III $$; and category IV $.

$$$$$

Cipriani, Giudecca 10, tel: 041-520 7744. On the island of Giudecca with private launch to run you to San Marco. The ultimate in luxury, with 54 rooms, 50 suites, luxuriant gardens and an Olympic-size pool (open April to December).
Hotel Danieli, Riva degli Schiavoni, 4196 Castello, tel: 041-522 6480. An old Gothic palazzo with 233 rooms and superb views across the lagoon. Dickens, Wagner, Ruskin and Balzac are among those who have stayed here.
Gritti Palace, Campo S Maria del Giglio, 2467 San Marco, tel: 041-794 611. Eighty-seven rooms in the former private palazzo of Doge Andrea Gritti

overlooking the Canal Grande. Room 10 is where Hemingway stayed. Generally considered to be the most exclusive hotel in Venice.
Palazzo Vendramin, Giudecca 10, tel: 041-520 7744. Superb 15th-century palace attached to the Cipriani: just 10 rooms and five suites. Individual butler service, stunning views over Venice and beautiful private gardens. Extremely expensive, but the ultimate in luxury and romance.

$$$$

Londra Palace, Riva degli Schiavoni, 4171 Castello, tel: 041-520 0533. Sixty-nine rooms and '100 windows overlooking the lagoon'. A comfortable, civilised hotel with club-style bar, French restaurant and excellent afternoon teas.

> ### Wheel your luggage
> Wheeled suitcases are extremely useful in Venice, as you will almost certainly be walking to your hotel. Porters are available at the station and the Piazzale Roma, but their fees are high, starting at €20,000 for taking one case into the city.

Luna Baglioni, Calle Vallaresso, 1243 San Marco, tel: 041-528 9840. The oldest hotel in Venice, founded in 1118 as a Knights Templar lodge for pilgrims travelling to Jerusalem. Extravagant decor (a riot of Murano glass and inlaid marble), an 18th-century ballroom and the grandest breakfast room in Venice.
Hotel Monaco & Grand Canal, Calle Vallaresso, 1325 San Marco, tel: 041-520 0211. Seventy-five rooms; exceptional setting on the Canal Grande. Open-air restaurant.

Saturnia & International, Calle Larga XXII Marzo, 2398 San Marco, tel: 041-520 8377. Ninety-five rooms in a 14th-century palazzo on a smart shopping street close to San Marco.

$$$

Abbazia, Calle Priuli dei Cavaletti, 66–8 Cannaregio, tel: 041-717 333. Converted monastery with 39 rooms and garden. Within easy reach of Piazzale Roma or the railway station.

Accademia Villa Maravege, Fondamenta Bollani, 1058–60 Dorsoduro, tel: 041-523 7846. Twenty-seven rooms in a quiet location close to the Accademia gallery, with views over the Canal Grande.

La Fenice et des Artistes. Campiello de la Fenice, 1936 San Marco, tel: 041-523 2333. Sixty-five rooms, many of which used to be taken by performers at the neighbouring Fenice opera house before the fire; still plenty of charm and character.

Flora, Calle Larga XXII Marzo, 2283A San Marco, tel: 041-520 5844. One of the most desirable small hotels in Venice with 44 rooms, pretty décor, quiet garden and location close to Piazza San Marco.

San Moisè, Calle del Cristo, 2058 San Marco, tel: 041-520 3755. Sixteen rooms, on canal near Fenice opera house. Small, friendly and quiet, with traditional Venetian-style fabrics and furnishings. Very convenient for Piazza San Marco. No restaurant.

Locanda Sturion, Calle Sturion, 679 San Polo, tel: 041-523 6243. Family-run guesthouse in a sumptuously decorated mansion. The Sturion is one of the oldest and most popular *locande*, beautifully situated near the Grand Canal and the Rialto. Eleven rooms.

$$–$

Agli Alboretti, Rio Terà Foscarini, 884 Dorsoduro, tel: 041-523 0058. Nineteen rooms. Simple and homely, close to Accademia gallery.

Bucintoro, Riva San Biagio, 2135 Castello, tel: 041-522 3240. Good-value, friendly *pensione* right on the waterfront near the Arsenale, with splendid views of the lagoon; 28 simple rooms, some without bathroom.

Calcina, Zattere, 780 Dorsoduro, tel: 041-520 6466. Thirty-seven rooms, many looking across the island of Giudecca. John Ruskin stayed here.

Paganelli, Riva degli Schiavoni, 4687 Castello, tel: 041-522 4324. Twenty-two rooms, three without bathroom. A modest, well-situated hotel, overlooking the lagoon and a quiet campo.

Peaceful backwaters

Locanda Fiorita, Campiello Nuovo, 3457 San Marco, tel: 041-523 4754. Ten rooms. Simple comforts and friendly service, on a small square behind Campo Santo Stefano.

Locanda Montin, Fondamento di Borgo, 1147 Dorsoduro, tel: 041-522 7151. Sited on the banks of a canal with a lovely garden, this *pensione* is very popular – advance booked recommended.

La Residenza, Campo Bandiera e Moro, 3608 Castello, tel: 041-528 5315. Fourteen rooms (some very small) in a handsome 15th-century palazzo overlooking a small square close to the Riva degli Schiavoni. Appeals to the independent traveller.

Hotel Alla Salute 'da Cici', Salute 222, Fondamente Ca' Balà, Dorsoduro, tel: 041-523 5404. This former palazzo is both characterful and well situated for the Basilica della Salute, the Accademia and the Guggenheim Collection. The rooms facing the quiet canal are especially attractive.

Seguso, Zattere, 779 Dorsoduro, tel: 041-528 6858. Thirty-six rooms. *Pensione* that appeals, particularly to British and French visitors, for its charm and splendid views across the Giudecca. Half-board only.

HOTELS ON THE LIDO
$$$$$
Westin Excelsior, Lungomare Marconi 41, tel: 041-526 0201. Large (191 rooms and three suites), five-star, modernised hotel by the beach close to the casino. Gardens, pool and tennis courts. Open mid-March to mid-November.

$$$$$
Grand Hôtel des Bains, Lungomare Marconi 17, tel: 041-526 5921. Four-star hotel across the road from the beach. Best known as the setting for the book and film of *Death in Venice* and still has an air of grandeur. Large gardens, swimming pool and tennis courts. Open March to November.

$$$
Villa Mabapa, Riviere San Nicolò 16, tel: 041-526 0590. Pleasant waterside location, convenient for the *vaporetti*; 68 rooms, attractive gardens.

$$
Biasutti (Villa Ada), Via E Dandolo 24, tel: 041-526 0120. A far cheaper alternative to the above. Three late-19th-century villas a few minutes from the beach.

YOUTH HOSTELS
Ostello di Venezia, Fondamenta Zitelle 86, Giudecca, tel: 041-523 8211, closed 16 January to 1 February. **Foresteria Valdese**, 5170 Castello (near S. M. Formosa), tel: 041-528 6797. Not an official youth hostel, but similar accomodation; book well in advance.

DAY HOTELS (ALBERGO DIURNO)
San Marco, Calle dell'Ascensione (near Piazza San Marco); and at the railway station (for showers only).

CAMPING
This is only possible on the mainland; the campsites tend to concentrate around the areas of Mestre-Marghera, Litorale del Cavallino and Chioggia.

> **Leave nothing to chance**
> As Venice is such a popular destination all year round, advance booking is not merely an option. If you know where you want to stay, book your accommodation as early as possible. Overbooking is sometimes a problem, especially in the smaller hotels, so it is wise to call to confirm your time of arrival.

✻ INSIGHT COMPACT GUIDES

Great Little Guides to the following destinations:

Algarve	Goa	St Petersburg	North York Moors
Amsterdam	Gran Canaria	Salzburg	Northumbria
Athens	Greece	Shanghai	Oxford
Bahamas	Holland	Singapore	Peak District
Bali	Hong Kong	Southern Spain	Scotland
Bangkok	Ibiza	Sri Lanka	Scottish
Barbados	Iceland	Switzerland	Highlands
Barcelona	Ireland	Sydney	Shakespeare
Beijing	Israel	Tenerife	Country
Belgium	Italian Lakes	Thailand	Snowdonia
Berlin	Italian Riviera	Toronto	South Downs
Bermuda	Jamaica	Turkey	York
Brittany	Jerusalem	Turkish Coast	Yorkshire Dales
Bruges	Kenya	Tuscany	
Brussels	Laos	Venice	*USA regional*
Budapest	Lisbon	Vienna	*titles:*
Burgundy	Madeira	Vietnam	Boston
California	Madrid	West of Ireland	Cape Cod
Cambodia	Mallorca		Chicago
Chile	Malta		Florida
Copenhagen	Menorca	*UK regional*	Florida Keys
Costa Brava	Milan	*titles:*	Hawaii – Maui
Costa del Sol	Montreal	Bath &	Hawaii – Oahu
Costa Rica	Morocco	Surroundings	Las Vegas
Crete	Moscow	Belfast	Los Angeles
Cuba	Munich	Cambridge &	Martha's Vineyard
Cyprus	Normandy	East Anglia	& Nantucket
Czech Republic	Norway	Cornwall	Miami
Denmark	Paris	Cotswolds	New Orleans
Dominican	Poland	Devon & Exmoor	New York
Republic	Portugal	Edinburgh	San Diego
Dublin	Prague	Glasgow	San Francisco
Egypt	Provence	Guernsey	Washington DC
Finland	Rhodes	Jersey	
Florence	Rio de Janeiro	Lake District	
French Riviera	Rome	London	
		New Forest	

Insight's checklist to meet all your travel needs:

- *Insight Guides* provide the complete picture, with expert cultural background and stunning photography. Great for travel planning, for use on the spot, and as a souvenir. 180 titles.
- *Insight Pocket Guides* focus on the best choices for places to see and things to do, picked by our correspondents. They include large fold-out maps. More than 120 titles.
- *Insight Compact Guides* are fact-packed books to carry with you for easy reference when you're on the move in a destination. More than 130 titles.
- *Insight Maps* combine clear, detailed cartography with essential information and a laminated finish that makes the maps durable and easy to fold. 125 titles.
- *Insight Phrasebooks* and *Insight Travel Dictionaries* are very portable and help you find exactly the right word in French, German, Italian and Spanish.

The world's largest collection of visual travel guides and maps

INDEX